C000004968

FOLLOWING THE TRAIL OF
TROOPER ALFRED PRIDE

Buffalo Soldier (1865–1893)

A Patriot and A Pawn

Dr. Alfred O. Taylor, Jr.

Following the Trail of Trooper Alfred Pride
© 2022 by Dr. Alfred O. Taylor, Jr.

All rights reserved. This book or any portion thereof may not be reproduced or used in any manner whatsoever without the express written permission of the publisher except for the use of brief quotations in a book review.

ISBN: 978-1-66783-390-3

FOREWORD

In the hands of a skilled historian, facts don't eclipse or replace imagination; they awaken it. Between the bricks in the wall of what is *known* about the past, there are openings, small windows that look beyond the facts of the story, into its beating heart.

Virginia is blessed with many fine historians who learned the craft of history not in classrooms or from any formal training but by listening to the sounds of voices speaking directly to them, sometimes through family lore and oral tradition and sometimes out of old documents—letters, photographs, and records of all kinds.

These "untrained" historians do what they do not to advance a career, make a living, or gain notoriety for themselves. They do it out of love: love for their people—family, neighbors, friends; for the places they come from and the stories they heard growing up; and to make sure the memories of these people and places, the stories, the lives—and the pieces of history they embody—are not lost. They learn the skills they need to learn along the way. Alfred Taylor, Jr. is one of these historians, and one of the best.

I first met Dr. Taylor more than ten years ago, in Arlington, Virginia. He was a legend even then. People told me: "if you want to know *anything* about African American life in Arlington, you have to talk to Dr. Taylor: you won't find anybody who knows more." And they were right.

Our first meeting was at Busboys and Poets in Shirlington. We saw each other a few times after that; gradually, we became confident with each other; we became friends. A year or two later, Virginia Humanities awarded a grant to support the publication of a landmark book Dr. Taylor had been working on called *Bridge Builders of Nauck/Green Valley*.

It's a carefully researched and loving account, honoring the people and places of one of Arlington's historically Black neighborhoods, a neighborhood that's changing very quickly now, the victim of "development" pressures—an old, familiar story, especially where Black neighborhoods are concerned.

Bridge Builders is a window, mostly looking back. It leaves the more difficult questions about what's happening to Nauck/Green Valley in the present (mostly) unaddressed. But his newest book, the book you're holding now, is different.

For one thing, it's more personal. It recounts what's known, or can be surmised, about his great grandfather Trooper Alfred Pride who served with the most decorated company of the legendary Buffalo Soldiers. Half the book is biography; but the other half delves deep into the heart of American history, the most troubled pieces of our American story.

Weaving these two strands together, *Following the Trail of Trooper Alfred Pride* is a work of personal courage, diligent research, love, frustration, and nearly universal appeal. Universal because while the story of this group Black soldiers might seem on the surface like an interesting but obscure chapter in our nation's history, in fact it lies at the core of that history, the heart of what made the United States what it is—and Americans who we are. And Trooper Alfred Pride, Dr. Taylor's great grandfather, lived that story every step of the way.

In the decades following emancipation, Black soldiers weren't allowed to serve in active duty anywhere east of the Mississippi, so great was the fear in many White Americans, that armed Black men posed a danger. So, the Buffalo Soldiers were given the task of supporting westward expansion; at the same time, their own dreams of owning land were being denied and betrayed.

From the Great Plains to the Rio Grande Valley—the West Texas Panhandle and the Oklahoma Territory to the Dakotas—these men were deployed at various times to protect White settlers, railroad crews, and surveying parties; recover stolen livestock, escort wagon trains, build roads, string telegraph lines, explore and map large areas of the uncharted West; and to carry the "flag" of Manifest Destiny, literally and symbolically, against Native peoples who were seen as standing in the way.

The "irony of African American soldiers fighting Native people on behalf of a government that accepted neither group as equals" is a vein that runs throughout this book—and through Trooper Pride's own life story.

The Buffalo Soldiers were crucial actors in the U.S. Government's campaigns against the Kiowa, Comanche, Apache, and a dozen other "hostile" Native tribes. They fought bravely and endured hardships that are difficult for us now to even imagine; and yet they still faced vicious hatred—racism—wherever they went.

As good as they were as soldiers, helping to quell Indian "resistance" and smooth the road for "settlement" of Native lands by Whites, there's another shard of irony in the story. When the Buffalo Soldiers were sent into Oklahoma Territory to protect the Indians who had been confined there from encroachment by White settlers on what were supposed to be protected lands, "Whites in the region quickly grew to detest these Black cavalrymen:" and violence committed *by* the White setters against Buffalo Soldiers was common.

The basic facts of Trooper Pride's service are known, but details are scant. Still, it's easy to imagine him as a young man born in Amelia Courthouse, Virginia, lying about his age so he could join the Army at the age of fifteen; enduring long days on horseback or the drill fields at Fort Sill, Fort Stockton, and Fort Concho; waiting in ambush for the legendary Apache warrior Victorio at a remote spring in West Texas; and fighting in the boiling sun along the Pecos River or being part of the last regiment to leave the site of the Wounded Knee massacre, in the Dakota winter.

Then later, on the train back east; ending his twenty-seven years of military service at Fort Myer in Virginia; working as a day laborer, bartender, and construction worker in Washington, D.C. where he died in 1910; and now lying in his well-earned final resting place, Section 23, Site 16813, at Arlington National Cemetery. A full life, except when his service is measured against the racism he and his fellow soldiers endured.

Imagination and nagging questions. There's a haunting photograph of eighteen men from Troop K, 9th Cavalry, which was Trooper Pride's Company. The men in the photo aren't identified: could one of them be Alfred Pride? And then another photograph, this one of the entire Company: which one is he?

It's impossible to know. The same way we can never know what he was thinking or how he felt waiting for that ambush, or when he was court-martialed (twice) for allowing a prisoner to escape. The first time, he was acquitted;

the second time, he was "busted" from sergeant down to private and forced to pay a fine but not punished any further because of his long service and the respect he had from his commanding officers. That much, at least, is documented.

We also know that Trooper Pride never received a pension of any kind for his service —nor did the other members of his Company. His widow did receive one, beginning six years after his death. But Trooper Pride never owned the land he hoped enlistment in the service of his country would one day enable him to purchase.

And so, the story of Trooper Alfred Pride is also an entry point, into a distinctively American saga, full of American sorrow, American shame; and into the forges of racism, bitter irony, and promises betrayed. It's a story of one group of people pitted against another—used as "pawns on a chessboard" by the perverse ideology that today we call "White supremacy."

Which is the thread that connects Trooper Pride's story to our lives in the present. And if you go back far enough, there's also a straight line connecting the fifteenth Century Doctrine of Discovery—in which the Catholic Church gave European powers the explicit authority to subjugate and, if necessary, eliminate Native inhabitants of the lands they "discovered"—all the way forward to the Buffalo Soldiers and to attempts at erasing Native cultural identity, both here in Virginia and across the United States.

Trooper Pride was part of a much larger story that touches the hot wires of cultural genocide; Black Codes, Jim Crow laws; vast disparities in the ways our nation's wealth are distributed; and the dissonance between American ideals and the hard truth of our collective past.

Still, and as his great grandson is quick to acknowledge, Trooper Pride was a *patriot*. He was also a man who lived a piece of American history that few of us know because we haven't been taught. *Following the Trail of Trooper Alfred Pride* is an important book about an American life. It's also a book about America itself, and one that, I hope, will inspire other great grandsons and great granddaughters to follow the trails of their own ancestors, so that we can all better understand where this country we love has come from; what it is; and what it can be.

David Bearinger

Palmyra, Virginia

February 5, 2022

WHY DID I WRITE THIS BOOK FROM TWO PERSPECTIVES?

I originally intended to write about my great grandfather Alfred Pride's career after my niece while tracing the ancestry of our maternal family discovered that he served in the Army (Buffalo Soldier), from 1865 until his retirement in 1893. Being a lover of history and having read about the accomplishments of the Buffalo Soldiers during the Indian Wars and with a new-found pride (no pun intended), I commenced on an effort to personalize his heroics and those of the units he was assigned to. Because there were many accounts of the Buffalo Soldiers heroics written, I thought writing it from a personal perspective would present a different point of view of their service, hardships, and extreme racism. My driving force was to publish an accounting for future generations of our family. The research of his tenure led me to rethink the single focus of my book, especially considering the Black Lives Matter movement, which was boosting the need for reparation and creating an environment of rapidly growing support.

Having heard and read about the Native Americans receiving some reparations through the Indian Claims Commission, land returns, and other outlets enticed me to further question whether the Buffalo Soldiers were deliberately led to believe that their newly found freedom would allow them to eventually own their land, only to later find out it was never to be. Starting with the Homestead Act of 1862 of which no Mexican, Native or African American could be a part of (they could not be citizens) gave White citizens or future White citizens up to 160 acres of public land provided they live on it and pay a small registration fee. The relationship to land—who owns it, who works it, and who cares for it—reflects obscene levels of inequality and legacies of colonialism and white supremacy in the United States, and elsewhere in the world.

To acquire the lands, the United States needed the help of the Buffalo Soldiers to help force the Indians to move from their homelands in the name of the "Manifest Destiny." It was needed to provide the public land for the westward movement. The Black troopers' dedication to their mission would easily classify them as Patriots. While on the other hand, it also revealed how they and the Native Americans were used as pawns by the U.S. Government. The second part focuses on land that was promised, given, and taken back.

INTRODUCTION TO PART ONE

Shortly after the Civil War, the thirty-ninth Congress on July 28, 1866 authorized the formation of the 9th and 10th Calvary and the 38th, 39th, 40th, and 41st Infantry Regiments: Six all-Black peacetime units. My great grandfather, Alfred Pride who was born in Amelia Court House, VA, near Richmond, ran away from home and changed his birth date (1851) to 1846 and enlisted in 1865 in Washington, D.C. (Source VA File WC 10020).

He was assigned to The Fortieth Infantry Regiment that was first organized September 5, 1866, in Washington, D.C., by Colonel Nelson Miles. Miles was a Civil War veteran of Fredericksburg, Antietam, and Chancellorsville. He later moved his headquarters to Camp Distribution, Virginia, in November 1866. (Source: Buffalo Soldiers: The Formation of the Twenty-Fourth).

In 1868 after his enlistment in the infantry for three years, he re-enlisted (five years) and was assigned to the Tenth Cavalry, Company B. He retired at Ft. Myer, Virginia, in 1893 as a member of the historic Ninth Cavalry, Company K.

During the Indian Wars of 1867–1891, the Ninth and Tenth Calvary participated in eleven campaigns against hostile Indians, among who were included Kiowas, Comanches, Utes, Cheyennes, Arapahoes, Kikapoos, Apaches, and Sioux. They were engaged in over 125 recorded skirmishes and battles, most of them in Texas and New Mexico, and including actions in Kansas, Oklahoma, Colorado, Arizona, Wyoming, the Dakotas, Idaho, Montana, and Mexico. Some were major engagements, but many were detachments actions in which noncommission officers held the command, and there were many examples of hardships withstood and heroism displayed. Other duties included guarding the border, apprehending bandits and cattle thieves, and maintaining order in sparsely and unruly territory.

(Source: Highland Falls the Town of Highlands)

Author's Note - I am assuming that my great grandfather, Alfred Pride who enlisted in the regular army in 1865 and served with the Ninth and Tenth Cavalry in addition to the 24th Infantry until his retirement in 1893, participated in many of these skirmishes and battles during his tenure. Unfortunately, until recently, little had been written about the Buffalo Soldiers before the Spanish American War because the Army did not require units to write regimental historical reports until the twentieth century. The few that were written vary widely in content and quality. Nevertheless, the information in them, when supplemented with other writings, can provide a complete account of Black regimental activities from 1865 to 1893. What follows is my attempt to provide a summary record of my great grandfather's achievements and service during those years by tracing records of his many enlistments with his assigned unit's involvement in a skirmish or battle and assume that he was a participant.

PROUD LEGACY OF THE BUFFALO SOLDIERS

In 1866, an Act of Congress created six all-Black peacetime regiments and later consolidated into four--the 9th and 10th Cavalry, and the 24th and 25th Infantry--who became known as "The Buffalo Soldiers." There are differing theories regarding the origin of this nickname. One is that the Plains Indians who fought the Buffalo Soldiers thought that their dark, curly hair resembled the fur of the buffalo. Another is that their bravery and ferocity in battle reminded the Indians of the way buffalo fought. Whatever the reason, the soldiers considered the name high praise, as buffalo were deeply respected by the Native peoples of the Great Plains. And eventually, the image of a buffalo became part of the 10th Cavalry's regimental crest.

According to HistoryNet: Buffalo Soldiers in Black History states 'Buffalo Soldiers' caught on with White journalists after it was first recorded in a letter to _The Nation_ in 1873. Plains Indians, the writer explained, coined it to describe 10th Cavalry troopers at Fort Sill. By 1879, an editor in New Mexico Territory had extended the term to the 9th Cavalry, and in 1894 the *Army and Navy Journal*, a privately owned but semiofficial weekly paper, included the infantry. (Frederic Remington had already given the term national circulation in 1889 with his article 'A Scout with the Buffalo Soldiers.') But Black soldiers themselves never seem to have used it in their letters to Black newspapers, in court-martial testimony or in pension applications. Among them, 'buffalo' was an insult, as when one soldier remarked that an officer 'had the men out on drill the other day, and he cursed one of the men, and they stood it like black buffalo sons of bitches.' Another private called a sergeant a 'God damned black, cowardly, buffalo son of a bitch.' Such language was the stuff of court-martial offenses, and trial transcripts recorded the men's words. Although many Black Regulars had great racial as well as professional pride, they did not express it by a nickname. 'Buffalo soldiers' seems to have been a term that appealed to outsiders, but insiders did not use.

Initially, the Buffalo Soldier regiments were commanded by Whites, and African American troops often faced extreme racial prejudice from the Army establishment. Many officers, including George Armstrong Custer, refused to command Black regiments, even though it cost them promotions in rank. In addition, African Americans could only serve west of the Mississippi River, because many Whites didn't want to see armed Black soldiers in or near their communities. And in areas where Buffalo Soldiers were stationed, they sometimes suffered deadly violence at the hands of civilians.

The Buffalo Soldiers' main duty was to support the nation's westward expansion by protecting settlers, building roads and other infrastructure, and guarding the U.S. mail. They served at a variety of posts in the Southwest and Great Plains, taking part in most of the military campaigns during the decades-long Indian Wars--during which they compiled a distinguished record, with eighteen Buffalo Soldiers awarded the Medal of Honor. This exceptional performance helped to overcome resistance to the idea of Black Army officers, paving the way for the first African American graduate from West Point Military Academy, Henry O. Flipper.

Much attention is given to the irony of African American soldiers fighting native people on behalf of a government that accepted neither group as equals. But at the time, the availability of information was limited about the extent of the U.S. Government's often-genocidal polices toward Native Americans. In addition, African American soldiers had recently found themselves facing Native Americans during the Civil War, when some tribes fought for the Confederacy.

(National Museum of African American History and Culture)

BOOK DESCRIPTION

The book is sectioned in two parts. The first part deals with the career of my great grandfather Trooper Alfred Pride and his service in the U.S. Army (Buffalo Soldiers) from 1865 until his retirement in 1893, in which I will declare was an act of Patriotism and Heroism by he and the African American Troopers. The second part of the book deals with how the African American Troopers, as well as the Native Americans, were used as "Pawns" to complete the belief by the European settlers and the U.S. Government that they were acting in accordance with the "Discovery Doctrine."

✳ ✳ ✳

ACKNOWLEDGMENTS

I acknowledge my niece Marcia Chapman who was my inspiration to become interested in pursuing the military career of my great grandfather when she started studying my mother's family and discovered the information about his service with the Buffalo Soldiers. I thank her for supplying me with the materials included as exhibits.

I also want to thank David Bearinger of the Virginia Foundation for the Humanities for encouraging me to start putting into writing all the stories of people's lives and their contributions that I usually presented in an oral medium. He would constantly remind me "you can write about everybody else's history, who's going to write yours?"

CONTENTS

CHAPTER 1
1865–1868

40th Infantry Regiment

Shortly after the Civil War, the thirty-ninth Congress on July 28, 1866 authorized the formation of the 9th and 10th Calvary and the 38th, 39th, 40th, and 41st Infantry Regiments: Six all-Black units. The U.S. Congress declared the Buffalo Soldiers as peacetime regiments consisting of African Americans only and being part of the regular U.S. Army. The six regiments were authorized to be manned by Black soldiers, but by 1869, there was a downsizing of all troops, and the Black regiments were cut down to two Infantry regiments and two cavalry regiments. (Source: HistoryNet).

My great grandfather, Alfred Pride was born in Amelia Court House, VA, near Richmond and ran away from home and changed his birth date (1851) to 1846 and enlisted in 1865 in Washington, D.C. (Source VA File WC 10020). Limited by education, training, and the social and economic barriers raised by American society, few Black men in the nineteenth century had advanced much beyond the status of unskilled laborers. I found no record of his education or training, but his enlistment stated "farmer."

The Fortieth Infantry Regiment was first organized September 5, 1866, in Washington, D.C., by Colonel Nelson Miles. Miles was a veteran of Fredericksburg, Antietam, and Chancellorsville. He later moved his headquarters to Camp Distribution, Virginia, in November 1866. (Source: Buffalo Soldiers: The Formation of the Twenty-Fourth).

The recruits from Washington, D.C. and Baltimore, Maryland, were assigned to the 40th Infantry and sailed from Alexandria, Virginia to the Carolinas where the rest of the regiment was organized. Indeed, several of the Blacks, many of whom previously had been slaves, joined the Army as a potential avenue to advancement and adventure. They saw the Army as a means to economic or social betterment. Perhaps the promise of education also motivated some knowledge-thirsty men, particularly after the Freedmen's Bureau, which had established schools for Blacks, shut down in 1866. Individuals who had been displaced by the Civil War could find food, shelter, clothing, and, to some extent, medical benefits by entering the military.

During the next two years, the regiments companies were stationed at sundry post in North and South Carolina (Forts Macon, Hatteras, Fisher, Caswell, Kinston, Plymouth, and Goldsboro in North Carolina, and Castle Pinckney, Walterboro, Orangeburg, and Hilton Head in South Carolina), never staying at one location more than a few months. In 1868, the Army consolidated the regiment in North Carolina, assigning the companies at Goldsboro and Raleigh. (Nankivell, 1972: 7–9).

Later, the 40th left North Carolina by rail to join the 39th Infantry at the Greenville Encampment in Louisiana. A year later, the new 25th Infantry formed at Jackson Barracks in New Orleans took ship for Texas where it served for the next ten years. (Source: HistoryNet).

Internet Content 2020 – Public Domain

Unknown 24th Infantry Company

CHAPTER 2
1868–1873

10ᵗʰ Cavalry Company B

At the expiration of his service at Fort Gibson, Indian Territory, he enlisted on February 10ᵗʰ, 1868 in Boston, Massachusetts, and was assigned to 10ᵗʰ Cavalry, Company B.

> **FORT GIBSON**—Fort Gibson remained a military post after the Civil War, but in 1871, most troops were transferred, leaving only a detachment responsible for provisions in a quartermaster depot. (Source: Wikipedia).

The 10th Cavalry was created in August 1866 and organized at Fort Leavenworth, Kansas. Recruiting the necessary men was especially slow, however. Four months after its creation, the 10th Cavalry consisted of only three officers and 64 "unassigned recruits" (Bigelow 1899: p. 299; Glass 1972: p. 13). The recruiting was so slow because men were selected specifically for these units by the Regiments officers (Bigelow 1899: p. 289). After several months of disappointing results from recruiting stations in the upper South, officers were sent to the northern cities of Boston, New York, Philadelphia, and Pittsburgh (Leckie 1967: p. 13). It was in Boston, Massachusetts that my great grandfather re-enlisted after serving three years in the infantry.

> **FORT LEAVENWORTH**—Fort Leavenworth was the base of African American soldiers of the U.S. 10th Cavalry Regiment of the U.S. Army, formed on September 21, 1866 at Fort Leavenworth. They became known as Buffalo Soldiers, nicknamed by the Native American tribes whom they fought. The term eventually was applied to all the African American regiments formed in 1866. (Source: Wikipedia).

The 10th Regimental's mission in Texas was to protect mail and travel routes, control Indian movements, provide protection from Mexican revolutionaries and outlaws, and gain knowledge of the area's terrain. African American regiments in the U.S. Army consistently received some of the worst duties the Army had to offer. For over two decades, the Ninth and Tenth Cavalry campaigned on the Great Plains, along the Rio Grande, in New Mexico, West Texas, Arizona, Colorado, and the Dakotas.

The Buffalo Soldiers endured unimaginable hardships from the overwhelming heat of the desert to the subfreezing temperatures of winter on the plains. Disease resulting from unsanitary conditions and inadequate provisions claimed the lives of many Black soldiers. They fought fierce Indian tribes, Mexican revolutionaries, cattle thieves, and outlaws while constantly receiving inferior horses, supplies, and equipment. They endured long, arduous expeditions over some of the roughest terrain in the country, searching for water sources, and mapping unknown terrain. (Source: A Fight for Freedom by Dave Bieri).

The regiment proved highly successful in completing their mission. The 10th scouted 34,420 miles (55,390 km) of uncharted terrain, opened more than 300 miles (480 km) of new roads, and laid over 200 miles (320 km) of telegraph lines. (Source: Buffalo Soldiers in Black History).

The scouting activities took the troops through some of the harshest and most desolate terrain in the nation. These excursions allowed the preparation of excellent maps detailing scarce water holes, mountain passes, and grazing areas that would later allow for settlement of the area. These feats were accomplished while the troops had to be constantly on the alert for quick raids by the Apaches. The stay in west Texas produced tough soldiers who became accustomed to surviving in an area that offered few comforts and no luxuries for those who survived.

On January 13, 1869, he was transferred to Fort Lyon, Colorado and assigned to the 10th Cavalry, Company K.

> **FORT LYONS**—Founded initially in 1867 as a U.S. Army Post, Fort Lyon was a military-related site until its transfer to the State of Colorado's Department of Corrections in the year 2000. As an Army fort, a navy hospital, and a Veteran's Administration hospital complex, Fort Lyon was in active service to one or more branches of the U.S. military for 133 years. Several companies of African American soldiers were quartered here in anticipation of General Philip Sheridan's winter campaign against the southern Cheyenne in 1868. (Source: Wikipedia).

The companies at Fort Lyon did not see any combat but made long marches under blizzard conditions that kept the various tribes from moving north or west. The troopers stationed in Indian Territory, on the other hand, experienced the same blizzard conditions but also engaged the Indians (Leckie 11967: pp. 39–44).

He was transferred to Fort Stockton and assigned to 10th Cavalry, Company B from January 14, 1869 until February 11, 1869.

> **FORT STOCKTON**—This important Indian Wars Fort was active from 1867 to 1886. It was strategically placed at the life-saving waters of Comanche Springs to protect the San Antonio-to-El Paso mail, freight wagons, cattle drives, and emigrants. The fort was garrisoned by the 9th Cavalry, known as "Buffalo Soldiers." It also provided employment for freighters and laborers and a market for farmers, stockmen, and merchants.(Source: Wikipedia).

He arrived at Post on June 14, 1869. He was assigned to 10th Cavalry, Company B, but was on extra duty when his company marched to Medicine Buff Creek from Ft. Dodge.

A movement of troops was now under way looking to a transfer of the regiment to the Department of Texas, and the end of April found Troops E, I, and L at Fort Richardson, Texas; and Troops C, D, and F enroute, the two former for Fort Griffin, the latter for Fort Concho, Texas. The headquarters were reestablished at Fort Sill on the 4th of May 1873 and remained there until the 27th of March 1875. During this time, the regiment continued serving partly in Texas and partly in the Indian Territory. The troops that were serving in the Indian Territory took part in the campaign of 1874–1875 against the Kiowas and Comanches. This campaign was but a continuation of the campaign of 1867–1868 and, like the latter, was directed by General Sheridan. There were four columns in the field operating separately under the following commanders:

Lieut. Colonel Neill, 6th Cavalry; Colonel N. A. Miles, 5th Infantry; Lieut. Colonel Davidson, 10th Cavalry; Colonel R. S. Mackenzie, 4th Cavalry.

Internet Content 2020 – Public Domain

Tenth Cavalry Unit Company B (Year Unknown)

Transferred to Fort Sill, Indian Territory. (Source: Special order 57 HQ Det 10 Cavalry. Camp Supply, Indian Territory August 10, 1969).

FORT SUPPLY—Fort Supply (originally Camp Supply) was a U.S. Army post established on November 18, 1868, in Indian Territory to protect the Southern Plains. It was located just east of present-day Fort Supply, Oklahoma, in what was then the Cherokee Outlet. (Source: Wikipedia).

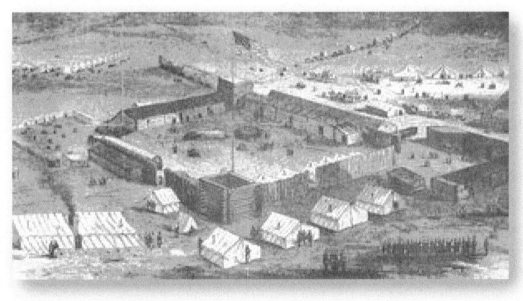

Camp Supply Stockade, *Harper's Weekly*, February 1869

Battle of Camp Supply (June 11, 1870)

Barely eighteen months had passed since the establishment of Camp Supply in the valley created by the confluence of Beaver River and Wolf Creek. The supply depot for General Philip Sheridan's winter campaign of 1868–1869 had grown to a garrison of five companies of the Tenth U.S. Cavalry and three of the Third Infantry. In the late spring of 1870, there were two camps, with about six hundred yards distance separating the commands of the two regiments.

The older of the two camps was as a rambling arrangement of log buildings and tents that had sprung up around the fortified stockade built in November 1868. To the southwest was the more orderly compound of log buildings. African American troopers of the Tenth had built picket-style log structures around a cavalry-sized quadrangle parade ground. On the west side were the stables for the cavalry horses. The garrison consisted of White officers and African American troopers of five troops of the Tenth: A, F, H, I, and K. Three companies of the Third—B, E, and F—were carried on the monthly returns of the post. The fighting ended as abruptly as it had begun. As with many of the long-range, running fights of the Indian Wars period, the number of combatants engaged, and the number of casualties were light. Two cavalry horses were wounded. A bugler captured an Indian pony and let one of the dismounted troopers ride it back to camp. No troops were killed or wounded. The official report listed six warriors killed and more wounded. Several wounded Indian ponies were captured. The warriors remained in the area for several days to harass the garrison. They fired into camp from nearby hills and killed a group of woodcutters north of the camp.

Nelson requested additional troops be sent to aid in the defense of the post, as he believed that the region would soon be engulfed in war that summer and fall. His request was denied, and the depredations during the next few weeks were minor. The flurry of incidents in May and early June that seemed a precursor of a major uprising proved to be the end of hostilities in the region. Fighting on that scale did not return to the region until the Red River War of 1874–1875.

The Battle of Camp Supply was the largest, most serious encounter in western Indian Territory between late 1868 and 1874. It demonstrated to the allied tribesmen that it would take more and bolder fighting to intimidate or defeat the army.

> **FORT SILL**—The site of Fort Sill was staked out on 8 January 1869 by Maj. Gen. Philip H. Sheridan, who led a campaign into Indian Territory to stop tribes from raiding border settlements in Texas and Kansas. (Source: Wikipedia).

Only occasionally was Fort Sill attacked. More frequently, army brass deemed "a show of force" necessary and ordered the 10th Cavalry to patrol the field, periodically for weeks at a time (Leckie 1967: pp. 45–61). Sheridan's massive winter campaign involved six cavalry regiments accompanied by frontier scouts such as Buffalo Bill Cody, Wild Bill Hickok, Ben Clark, and Jack Stilwell. Troops camped at the location of the new fort included the 7th Cavalry, the 19th Kansas Volunteers and the 10th Cavalry, a distinguished group of Black "buffalo soldiers" who constructed many of the stone buildings still surrounding the old post quadrangle. (Source: Wikipedia). From Fort Sill, the regimental headquarters moved back to Fort Gibson. They left Fort Sill on the 5th of June 1872. During the three years and two months of their stay at that station, most of the regiment—for a time there were eleven troops—was constantly at headquarters.

In June 1872, the army transferred the 10th Cavalry headquarters back to Fort Gibson in response to an increase in the number of White intruders into Indian Territory from the north. Less than a year later, regimental headquarters returned to Fort Sill.

FORT GIBSON—In 1872, the 10th Cavalry reoccupied Fort Gibson. Soon after, workers were sent to the area to build the Missouri–Kansas–Texas Railroad from Baxter Springs, the first "cow town," in Kansas, to the Red River crossing at Colbert's Ferry, Indian Territory, along the Texas border. This would improve transportation of cattle and beef to the east as well as shipping of goods from that area to the West. The cavalry from Fort Gibson was used to police the camps of local workers. Soldiers tried to manage threats from outlaws, White encroachment on Indian lands, intra-tribal disputes, and other issues. The size of the garrison varied with the workload. (Source: Wikipedia)

Fort Gibson in northeastern Oklahoma saw the arrival of Buffalo Soldiers in April 1867. They served there between 1867 and 1869 and from 1872 until 1873 with the post designated as the headquarters of the 10th U.S. Cavalry from 1868 until 1873.

CHAPTER 3
1873–1878

10th Cavalry, Company B

In spring of 1873, companies of the 10th were transferred to Texas to forts Richardson, Griffin and Concho (Company B went to Fort Griffin). At various times, Buffalo Soldiers of the 9th and 10th Cavalry regiments served at virtually every Texas frontier fort from the Rio Grande to the Red River and on into the Panhandle. The proud Black troops built and renovated dozens of forts, strung thousands of miles of telegraph lines, and escorted wagon trains, stagecoaches, railroad trains, cattle herds, railroad crews, and surveying parties. They opened new roads and mapped vast areas of the West. They recovered thousands of head of stolen livestock for civilians, brought dozens of horse thieves to justice, and pursued Indian raiders, often having to stay on the move for months at a time. After Indians had been displaced from West Texas, the Buffalo Soldiers were assigned to pursue them into New Mexico, Colorado, and the Dakotas. They also earned the respect of many previously dubious army officers. (Written by Mary G. Ramos, editor emeriti, for the Texas Almanac 1990–1991).

THE COURT MARTIAL PROCEEDINGS OF ALFRED PRIDE FOR NEGLECT OF DUTY – June 28, 1873

Court Martial of Private Alfred Pride, Company B, 10th Cavalry, Fort Sill, Indian Territory. He was charged with "Neglect of duty, to the prejudice of good order and military discipline" Specification: "That Private Alfred Pride, Co. B, 10th Cavalry, having been duly placed as sentinel in charge of George Davis, Private of Co. I, 10th Cavalry, a general prisoner awaiting trial by general court martial for desertion, did allow said Davis to escape from him, said prisoner Davis being at the time shackled. This at Fort Gibson, Indian Territory on the 24th of March 1873. To which charge and specification the accused pleaded "Not Guilty" Finding: The court having maturely considered the evidence presented, finds the accused not guilty of the specification and not guilty of the charge. And the court does therefore acquit him. (See Exhibit 1)

COMPANY B MOVED TO FORT GRIFFIN

In April 1873, the army ordered companies south into Texas. Three companies were stationed at Fort Richardson, two at Fort Griffin, and two at Fort Concho. Troops A, F, G, I, and L, at Fort Concho; **B** and E at Fort Griffin; C and K at Fort McKavett; H at Fort Davis; D and M in the field at Buffalo Springs, I.T. During the month of May, troops D and M moved from the Indian Territory, the former to Fort Concho, the latter to Fort Stockton.

FORT GRIFFIN—One of these new forts was Fort Griffin, which opened in 1867. It was built on top of a hill in the beautiful, scrubby countryside of Shackleford County to allow Texans to settle Comanche country. Along with Fort Richardson, which lay just to the northeast of Fort Griffin, these forts marked the boundary line of 'civilization' from Indian Territory all the way to the Rio Grande at Fort Davis. (Source: Wikipedia)

The Indian Territory was relatively quiet during the summer of 1873, although small raiding parties continued to harass the north Texas border (Wharfield 1965: pp. 55–57). The black troopers spent most of the summer in the saddle, scouting for these raiders, but saw little action (Leckie 1967: pp. 76–78).

FIRST CAPTURE OF CAMPAIGN – October 25, 1874

The first capture of the campaign was made by a portion of Davidson's column. On the 25th of October 1874, Troops **B** and M, 10th Cavalry, and one company of the 11th Infantry, under command of Major Schofield, while in pursuit of Indians near Elk Creek, pressed them so hard that the whole band surrendered. They numbered 68 warriors, 276 squaws and children, and about 1500 ponies. These prisoners, and others taken subsequently, were put in camp at Fort Sill, the more dangerous bucks being closely confined. At the close of the campaign the ringleaders were sent to Fort Marion, Florida, under charge of Captain Pratt. It was this action and others like it that helped gain the respect of American Indians and White officers for the Black American regular soldier. In his after-action report, Nelson wrote, "In the series of conflicts narrated above, I would invite special attention to the admirable conduct of the enlisted men. They justify every confidence and the splendid esprit exhibited by them making no question where victory will rest whatever the odds against them."

After the Red River Indian War (1874–1875), the 10th Cavalry was transferred to Texas, where the 9th Cavalry, commanded by Colonel Edward Hatch, had long been based. The combined forces fought outlaws and Indians who often conducted raids and robberies from sanctuaries in Mexico. They carried out a campaign against the Apache, who were resisting relocation and confinement on reservations. After numerous battles with Victorio and his Apache band, the soldiers managed to subdue them in 1880. While the 10th Cavalry continued in action against the remaining Apache for another decade, the 9th was sent to Indian Territory (later Oklahoma) to deal with Whites who were illegally settling on Indian lands. (Source: Buffalo Soldiers. U.S. Military).

When moved for the second time from Fort Sill, the regimental headquarters were transferred to Fort Concho, Texas, where they were established on April 17, 1875. The 1st of May found the troops of the regiment located in Texas and Indian Territory as follows: Six companies were assigned to Fort Concho, with two each at Forts Griffin and McKavett. And one each at Forts Davis and Stockton (Glass 1972: p. 20).

TROOP B CROSSING INTO MEXICO

In July 1876, Troops B, E, and K crossed into Mexico as part of a column commanded by Lieut. Colonel Shafter, 24th Infantry. A detachment of this command made up of twenty picked men of Troop B under Lieutenant Evans, and twenty Seminole scouts, all under command of Lieutenant Bullis, 24th Infantry, made a march of 110 miles in twenty-five hours and thereby succeeded in surprising a camp of twenty-three lodges of hostile Lipans and

Kickapoos near Saragossa, Mexico. They killed ten Indians, captured four, and captured about 200 horses. They then made a bonfire of the camp material and with their prisoners and captured stock rejoined the main column as fast as their jaded horses would carry them.

LETTER FOUND FROM PVT. ALFRED PRIDE TO GENERAL ORD AT FORT DUNCAN (1877)

In 1877, Lieutenant John Bigelow, Jr., a recent graduate of West Point was assigned to begin duty with Company B, 10th Cavalry at Ft Duncan, Texas. The book *Frontier Cavalryman* (pp. 60–61) reports that Alfred Pride with the assistance of Lt. John Bigelow at Fort Duncan, Texas wrote a letter of complaint to the paymaster about not receiving pay for six months. (Source: Kinevan). It stated:

Thursday, December 20, 1877 . . . I found a letter in my room, written for Private Alfred Pride to Gen'l Ord:

Sir.

I wish to inform the Gen'l Comd'g of the unjust manner in which I was treated. My company was paid (on) Decb'r 13ᵗʰ 1877. Being absent on detached service I was not paid . . . I presented myself to (the Paymaster) at 3 p.m. yesterday but he refused to pay me saying his safe was locked up. I have been nearly six months without pay and need the money, and request (it) . . . Be Sent to me in a check.

". . . [The letter] was not respectful enough to please me [Lt. Bigelow]. The signature was not prefixed by any remarks as to the respect in which the writer held the person addressed…Then the first sentence would give the impression that the writer had some personal ill feeling toward the paymaster instead of being simply desirous of obtaining his dues."

To remedy these shortcomings, Bigelow composed a highly stylized revision replete with obsequious salutations and the customary close from "your obedient servant." He neglected later to mention whether the impoverished Private Pride ever received his back pay.

On February 11, 1878, the 10ᵗʰ Cavalry, Company B left Fort Duncan, Texas. He was left at this fort with discharge for signature of commanding office and final statements completed and signed. On February 11, 1878, he was relieved of duty at that fort.

FORT DUNCAN—The Post was reoccupied by Federal troops in March 1868. In 1870, several Seminole Indians were working at the forts as guides and scouts. In 1883, the fort was once again abandoned because the site upon which it was located was leased and the owner wouldn't sell. (Source: Wikipedia).

CHAPTER 4
1878–1883

24th Infantry, Company F

On February 11, 1878, he enlisted at Fort Duncan and was assigned to the 24th Infantry, Company F and served in that unit until his discharge on February 10, 1883 at the expiration of his service at Fort Elliott, Texas.

24th INFANTRY, COMPANY F—The 24th Infantry Regiment (one of the Buffalo Soldier regiments) was organized on 1 November 1869 from the 38th U.S. (Colored) Infantry Regiment (formed 24 July 1866) and the 41st U.S. (Colored) Infantry Regiment (formed 27 July 1866). All the enlisted soldiers were Black, either veterans of the U.S. Colored Troops or freedmen. From its activation until 1898, the 24th Infantry served throughout the Western United States. Its missions included garrisoning frontier posts, battling American Indians, protecting roadways against bandits, guarding the border between the United States and Mexico. (Source: Wikipedia).

In 1878, a platoon of soldiers from the 24th Infantry was detailed to the 2nd Artillery and given extensive training to the operation of the Gatling gun. Col. Hunt and General Ord, commander of the Department of Texas, were impressed by the platoon's success with the gun, and by the gun's accuracy and mobility (Utley 1973: p. 73). The African American soldiers who tested the gun's operation apparently never got the chance to demonstrate their abilities in combat.

(The Army refused to create a Black artillery regiment because many believed Blacks were not intelligent enough to serve as artillerymen (Donaldson, 1991: p. 61; Nalty 1986: p. 51).

FORT ELLIOTT—Fort Elliott was the U.S. Army outpost in eastern Texas Panhandle from 1875 to 1890. Though never involved in a major military engagement, it helped transform the Panhandle from Indian hunting territory into a settlement area. Troops from Fort Elliott patrolled the borders of Indian Territory to the east, policed cattle drives headed north to Kansas railroad depots, and, in other ways, protected and encouraged settlement of the region. In 1879, a company of the Black Tenth U.S. Cavalry was assigned to the garrison, and between 1880 and 1888 other Black units, companies of the Twenty-fourth U.S. Infantry and Ninth U.S. Calvary served there. From November 1881 until February 1884, all of Fort Elliott's troops were Black. The commissioned officers were all White, however, except for Lt. Henry O. Flipper, the first Black graduate of West Point. Troops from Fort Elliott patrolled both the Panhandle and western Indian Territory. Their main task was to stop small hunting parties of Indians from entering the Panhandle, but on several occasions during the late 1870s, they pursued bands seeking to escape the reservation. (Source: Texas State Historical Association).

In 1878, the rest of the 24th Infantry moved up from the Rio Grande posts, back to Fort Davis, Stockton, and Concho. From these stations, four companies of the regiment took part in one more important campaign against the Texas Apaches (Utley 1973: p. 362). The "Victorio War of 1879–1880," long has been overshadowed by other Indian campaigns, probably due-to-the-fact that the Army failed in capturing or killing Victorio. They did confine Victorio to Mexico, where he was finally defeated.

Even less recognized is the role that Black infantrymen played in the Victorio Campaign. In fact, regimental history of the 24th Infantry does not even mention this campaign. Under the command of Colonel Benjamin Grierson during this campaign, infantrymen from the 24th served as camp guards and protected the supply train for the 10th Cavalry. (Leckie 1967: pp. 226–227).

On July 11, 1878, he enlisted at Fort Robinson, Nebraska at the expiration of his service at Fort Elliott. He was assigned to the 10th Cavalry, Company B.

FORT ROBINSON—Fort Robinson was a base of U.S. military forces and played a major role in the U.S. War of aggression against the native Sioux communities Sioux Wars from 1876 to 1890.

In January 1879, Chief Morning Star (also known as Dull Knife) led the Northern Cheyenne in an outbreak from the Agency. Because the Cheyenne had refused to return to Indian Territory, where they believed conditions were too adverse for them to survive, the army had been holding and starving them of food, water, and heat during the severe winter. This campaign of torture and neglect was a tactic to try to force them into submission. U.S. soldiers hunted down the escapees, killing men, women, and children in the Fort Robinson massacre. The U.S. Supreme Court described it as a "shocking story," "one of the most melancholy of Indian tragedies."[8] The event marked the end of the Sioux and Cheyenne wars in Nebraska. (Source: Wikipedia).

The Fort Robinson Massacre

The Fort Robinson tragedy (winter 1878–1879) refers to a series of events that occurred during the winter of 1878–1879 at Fort Robinson in northwestern Nebraska. After having been forced to relocate south to the Darlington Agency in the Southern Cheyenne Reservation, a band of Northern Cheyenne fled back north in September 1878 because of the terrible conditions. The U.S. Army intercepted part of the Northern Cheyenne Exodus and took a band of nearly 150 Cheyenne to Fort Robinson in Nebraska.

In January, after the Cheyenne had refused an earlier order to return to the south, the soldiers began to treat them more harshly to try to force them south: they were confined to a barracks without rations or wood for heat. Most of the band escaped on January 9, but the U.S. Army hunted them down. They quickly returned sixty-five to the Fort, and by January 22 cornered and killed most of the last thirty-two escapees, as they were poorly armed and greatly outnumbered by 150 soldiers. (Source: Wikipedia).

Tenth Cavalry in Victorio's War

May 1880: General Sheridan assigned Colonel Grierson's Tenth U.S. Cavalry to assist in the capture of Victorio. Instead of going into New Mexico, Colonel Grierson felt Victorio would come to Texas to raid. Grierson also decided to change his strategy in confronting Victorio. Instead of his men chasing Victorio across the desolate countryside, he would post them at the canyon passes and water holes he thought Victorio would use.

Victorio's War

Background Event: Chief Victorio also known as Apache Wolf, is considered one of the fiercest of the Apache. He and his Warm Springs Apaches left the hated San Carlos Reservation. He had done this twice before but had returned. When moved to Fort Stanton, New Mexico, he fled again, but this time he said, he would never return. Victorio reasoned that the arrival of the new judge and district attorney meant he would be tried for old murders and horse stealing. He and others also left, because government would not give them their promised food allotments, so they and their families were starving. Before Victorio's breakout, the heroic Ninth U.S. Cavalry had been given the distasteful task of returning Apaches who left their reservation. They also had to protect the Apaches on and off the reservation from cowboys and others who often hunted and killed Indians for sport. Some Whites made a living by selling Indian scalps to the Mexican Government who paid fifty dollars for a male, twenty-five dollars for a female and ten dollars for a child's scalp. At one time, the Apaches had been allowed to hunt under the protection of the military, but the settlers didn't like seeing armed Indians so the practice was discontinued. Colonel Hatch of the Ninth U.S. Cavalry, complained to General Sheridan that the Apaches were going to starve if they couldn't leave the reservation to hunt. Sheridan was not impressed with Hatch's letter.

September 4, 1879: Ojo Caliente, Arizona. As Victorio became more and more hate filled, he began to mutilate bodies. Soon after breaking out of the San Carlos Reservation, Victorio and the men struck at Captain Hooker and Company E of the Ninth stealing forty-six of their horses. In the aftermath, five Buffalo Soldiers lay dead with their bodies staked to the ground. They were Sergeant Silas Chapman, Privates Lafayerre Hoke, William Murphy, Silas Graddon, and Alvrew Percival. Victorio and his band escaped.

September 10, 1879: By this time, nine settlers had been killed by Victorio's band and other groups of Apaches had joined in the fighting. All the Ninth's Companies with Apache and Navaho scouts were in the field, always one step behind Victorio. Thousands of soldiers would continue this scenario for the next year, skirmishing Victorio's band over thousands of grueling miles, in the worst of conditions.

September 16, Black Range Mountains, New Mexico: Lieutenant Colonel Dudley with Captain Dawson's B Company and Hooker's E were ambushed and trapped by Victorio's warriors. They were rescued by Captain Beyer and Lieutenant Hugo of Companies C and G. After a day of fighting, the soldiers broke off the engagement. Five soldiers, three scouts and thirty-two horses lay dead after the bloody battle.

November 1879: The Candelaria Mountains, Mexico: Victorio and his warriors ambushed and killed fifteen Mexican citizens from the little village of Carrizal, who were looking for cattle thieves. Later, eleven more citizens were killed while searching for those what had not returned. The Mexican Government telegraphed the U.S. commander in the area, to inform him that they were after Victorio, which would probably drive him back into Texas.

January 9 to May 1880: Major Morrow, who had assumed command of operations in Southern New Mexico, sent the Buffalo Soldiers of the Ninth against Victorio's band many times during this period. In most of these cases, Victorio's war party fought off the soldiers. Sometimes, the fighting ended quickly. At other times, it lasted for long hours.

May 1880: General Sheridan assigned Colonel Grierson's Tenth U.S. Cavalry to assist in the capture of Victorio. Instead of going into New Mexico, Colonel Grierson felt Victorio would come to Texas to raid. Grierson also decided to change his strategy in confronting Victorio. Instead of his men chasing Victorio across the desolate countryside, he would post them at the canyon passes and water holes he thought Victorio would use.

May 12, Bass Canon west of Fort Davis: Eight Mescalero warriors attacked a wagon train killing two settlers and wounding two. Captain Carpenter of the Tenth U.S. Cavalry with Company H pursued them to the Rio Grande. He was convinced they were on their way to join Victorio.

Last of the Seminole

July 1880 Eagle Springs, Texas: Lieutenant Henry Flipper was the first Black officer in the U.S. military and the first to graduate from the West Point Military Academy. He was in charge of three troopers who rode ninety-eight miles in twenty-one hours to inform Captain Gillmore that Victorio's advance guard had been spotted. This information was forwarded to Colonel Grierson who thought Victorio and his warriors would head for Eagle Springs. His men marched sixty-eight miles in twenty-four hours to arrive there ahead of Victorio's band. To their disappointment, Victorio had turned northwest, heading for Rattlesnake Springs. That same night, they marched sixty miles more to Rattlesnake Springs.

Battle of Rattlesnake Springs

August 6, 1880, Rattlesnake Springs, Texas: Captain Viele was placed in charge of Companies C and G of the Tenth as they waited for Victorio's approach. At mid-afternoon, their long wait was rewarded. Slowly, Victorio's warriors advanced unaware of the ambush. Seconds before the signal to fire was given, Victorio sensed the danger and halted his men. The troopers opened fire. The warriors swiftly withdrew out of range. Needing water and believing there were only a few soldiers, Victorio immediately attacked. Carpenter and B and H companies counter attacked, temporarily halting the Indians advance. Meanwhile, a strong unit of Victorio's band struck at the army wagons that were in route to the springs. They were beaten off, and soon rejoined Victorio's contingent. Victorio's warriors repeatedly charged the troopers to reach the water. Finally, in near darkness, one last attempt was made to reach the spring. It failed and Victorio fled with the troopers in furious pursuit. The chase ended without further bloody contact. With Colonel Grierson's strategy in place, all mountain passes, and water holes were now covered by the troopers.

August 9th: Victorio's supply camp was discovered. His guards retreated, leaving twenty-five head of cattle, dried beef, and pack animals.

August 11, 1880: The Buffalo Soldiers with Captains Carpenter and Nolon found Victorio and his warriors. In the heat of the thunderous chase, the horses in Carpenter's Company gave out, leaving Nolon's troopers to continue the chase. Victorio's warriors crossed the Rio Grande River into Mexico before Nolon's troopers could catch them. Victorio, like many times before, had escaped. Thus ends the "Battle of Rattlesnake Springs." Soon after Victorio's return to Mexico, its government gave the U.S. military permission to cross into Mexico with the expressed intention of capturing Victorio dead or alive.

October 4, 1880: Ten companies of the Tenth U.S. Cavalry were placed inside Mexico at the Rio Grande to stop Victorio from returning into Texas. The Tenth and Colonel Jaoquin Terraza's Mexican forces located Victorio and his band. Five days later, the Mexican Government informed the American forces their presence in Mexico was no longer needed. The Buffalo Soldiers left under protest. Colonel Grierson asked General Sheridan for permission to return to Mexico, permission was denied.

October 14, 1880: Tres Castillos Mountains, Mexico; Colonel Terrazas and his Mexican troops surrounded Victorio's camp and attacked. Before the morning was over Victorio, sixty warriors and eighteen women and children lay dead. Sixty-eight women and children were taken prisoner.

Death road with Victorio, as silently as a shadow, when he and his warriors returned to Mexico. With Victorio's War at an end, the Trans-Pacos area was somewhat at peace. Colonel Grierson reported that during "Victorio's War," the Tenth U.S. Cavalry lost three troopers and saw three wounded. He also reported trooper Private Wesley Hardy as missing in action.

After completing this campaign, the Tenth was transferred to the Department of Arizona. They were engaged once again in a campaign against Apaches, who this time, was under the leadership of Chief Mangus and the Apache Kid. In September 1886, a detachment from the Tenth Cavalry captured Chief Mangus, the last of the war.

In the 1880's, the Oklahoma Territory was still used by the Federal government as a reservation for more than a dozen different Indian tribes. Whites were prohibited by law from entering the Indian Territory. Of course, this did not stop them from invading the Indians domain. Between 1879 and 1881, alarming numbers of settlers began filtering into Oklahoma (Leckie: 1967: pp. 246–247). To stem this tide of settlement, the Army sent the 9th Cavalry to Kansas and Oklahoma Territory. Instead of fighting Indians as they had in Texas and New Mexico, here the Buffalo Soldiers defended them by removing those squatters from their land. Whites in the region quickly grew to detest the Black cavalrymen. The soldiers' main mission was to secure the road from San Antonio to El Paso and restore and maintain order in areas disrupted by Native Americans, many of whom were frustrated with life on Indian reservations and broken promises by the federal government. The Black soldiers, facing their own forms of discrimination from the U.S. Government, were tasked with removing another minority group in that government's name.

CHAPTER 5
1883–1888

9th Cavalry, Company K

On March 10, 1883, he enlisted in St. Louis, Missouri and was assigned to the 9th Cavalry, Company K. until his discharge on March 9, 1888.

> **JEFFERSON BARRACKS MILITARY POST** – Located on the Mississippi River at Lemay, Missouri, south of St. Louis, Missouri. It was an important and active U.S. Army station from 1826 through 1946.

In the 1870s and the 1880s, the 9th Cavalry fought with great distinction throughout the western United States in numerous campaigns against marauding American Indians, Mexicans, and lawless settlers. In June 1881, the regiment was moved from New Mexico to Kansas and Indian Territory, where it remained until 1885. Most of these years were spent in garrison, though the intruders upon the Oklahoma Territory, which at that time was not open for settlement kept several of the troops busy moving over that country and patrolling the northern portion of Indian Territory and southern Kansas. The conditions the troopers fought in while chasing the Apache are described in a letter from Colonel Hatch to General Pope.

> *"The work performed by these troops is most arduous, horses worn to mere shadows, men nearly without boots, shoes and clothing. That the loss in horses may be understood when following the Indians in the Black Range. The horses were without anything to eat five days except what they nibbled from pinon pines, going on without food so long was nearly as disastrous as the fearful march into Mexico of 79 hours without water, all this by forced marches over inexpressibly rough trails. . . . It is impossible to describe the exceeding roughness of such mountains as the Black Range and the San Mateo. The well-known Modoc Lava beds are a lawn compared with them." (Hatch to Pope, February 25, 1880 – Source: Buffalo Soldiers, cavhooah.com).*

The 9th Cavalry was often the only source of security on the frontier and was often at odds with those who would profit from banditry. While most of the 9th Cavalry's actions were against hostile Indians, in 1884, the regiment also protected friendly Indian tribes settled in present day Oklahoma from settlers seeking to steal their land.

After warfare and work in New Mexico (1881), the army transferred the Ninth Cavalry to Indian Territory and assigned them the job of preventing Boomers from illegally moving from Kansas to Oklahoma. In the mid-1880s, more than 2,000 Boomers filtered in from various points along the border, requiring the constant attention of six companies of Black cavalrymen. African American soldiers drove out the majority of those already in Oklahoma, but as a result racism exploded. One officer was referred to as "one of a litter of mud turtles born of a Negro woman." The imposing and thankless task of driving Boomers from Indian Territory ended for the Ninth Cavalry in June 1885 when it was transferred to Wyoming.   Among other feats, Buffalo Soldiers in Indian Territory assisted local authorities and federal marshals, escorted civilians, stagecoaches, and freighters, guarded railroad construction workers and mail carriers, forestalled Boomers, chased robbers, horse thieves, and cattle rustlers, attempted pacification of Indians, and provided protection for Indians in Indian Territory.

In 1885, several companies from the 9th Cavalry were detailed to Indian Territory to remove the Boomers—White homesteaders who were trying to stake illegal claims on Indian lands.

In the summer of 1885, the regiment was moved to the Department of the Platte. Where it remained, enjoying a well-earned rest after the many scouts and campaigns of the preceding years.

In the 1800s, Black troops were not allowed on base at Fort D. A. Russell in Cheyenne, Wyoming due to segregation and limited space. The first Black troops stationed near the fort was Troop K, 9th Cavalry (my great grandfather's troop) who were ordered there by President Grover Cleveland to protect federal employees who were removing illegal fences. (Source: Historicwyoming.org/profiles/buffalosoldiersatfortdarussell).

FORT A. D. RUSSELL—The fort was established in 1867 to protect workers for the Union Pacific Railroad

Wikemedia – Public Domain
Troop K, Ninth Cavalry

All I Can Do Is Wonder Was He One of Those Pictured

CHAPTER 6
1888–1893

He reenlisted at Fort Robinson; Nebraska on March 10, 1888 and served until his discharge on March 9, 1893 at Fort Myer, Virginia at the expiration of his service.

Internet Content 2020 – Public Domain
A Ninth Cavalry squadron on the drill field, circa 1892-93. Each of the four troops has its own guidon and its own color of horse. The shadow of the reviewing stand is visible in the foreground; Crow Butte and a few of the Fort Robinson buildings are visible in the right background.

On July 1, 1888, Alfred Pride was appointed Sergeant, Company K/9th Calvary at Fort Robinson, Nebraska and served at that rank until court martialed in 1890 for letting a prisoner escape.

Swabuffalosoldiers.org

9th Cavalry Non-Commission Officers – 1889

Names of pictured unknown. Don't know if one of them is my great grandfather, but he was a Sergeant in Company K in 1889.

THE COURT MARTIAL PROCEEDINGS FOR ALLOWING A PRISONER TO ESCAPE – October 17, 1890

Charge: Sergeant Alfred Pride, Troop K, 9th Cavalry was charged with "Neglect of duty, in violation of the 62d Articles of War" "that he, Sergeant Alfred Pride, Troop K, 9th Cavalry, being duly detailed as sergeant of the post guard, did while in charge of said guard, permit Alfred Fowler, Company C, 8th Infantry, a prisoner to escape. This at Fort Robinson, Nebraska, and on or about the 2nd of October 1890.

Although he pleaded not guilty, he was found guilty and sentenced "To be reduced to the rank of private soldier, and to forfeit ten ($10.00) per month of his pay for two months. The court is thus lenient on account of his long service and good character as shown in evidence."

On November 18, 1890, Sergeant of the Guard, Alfred Pride was court martialed, when it was alleged that he allowed a prisoner to escape and was reduced to private and fined $20.00. "But for his long service and good character the sentence would have been more severe." (Source: ANJ 28) (18 November 1890): p. 120. [See transcript Exhibit 2]

The Battle at Pine Ridge, South Dakota

On December 30, 1890, Troop D under Captain Loud was attacked while escorting a wagon train near Pine Ridge Agency, South Dakota, losing one man killed. Later in the same day, Troops D, F, I, and K, under Major Henry, were engaged near the Drexel Mission, S.D., no casualties.

The 9th Cavalry's "one last moment of glory" in the old west was quelling the Sioux Ghost Dance uprising during the summer of 1890. (Leckie 1967: p. 252).

The War Department ordered an army buildup at the Pine Ridge Reservation (in present day South Dakota), and 500 to 600 hostile ghost dancers gathered. Tensions between the two groups, which included the buffalo soldiers of the Ninth Calvary, resulted in the Wounded Knee Massacre on December 28. More than 150 Sioux were killed. After that the Ghost Dance movement waned. (Source Wikipedia).

GHOST DANCE—The Ghost Dance was a new religious movement incorporated into numerous Native American belief systems. According to the teachings of the Northern Paiute spiritual leader Wovoka (renamed Jack Wilson), proper practice of the dance would unite the living with spirits of the dead, bring the spirits to fight on their behalf, make White colonists leave, and bring peace, prosperity, and unity to Native American people throughout the region. (Source Wikipedia).

Major Guy V. Henry and the 9th Cavalry's Great Cavalry Ride (The Greatest Ride in Cavalry History)

The battalion of the 9th Cavalry was scouting near the White River (Missouri River tributary) about fifty miles north of Indian agency at Pine Ridge when the Wounded Knee Massacre occurred. Troops D, F, I, and K of the 9th Cavalry, under the command of Major Guy V. Henry, made a forced march in harsh winter conditions to the Pine Ridge Agency from Fort McKinney, Nebraska, to Pine Ridge, South Dakota. It was one of the greatest cavalry rides in recorded military history. The 9th Cavalry arrived at Wounded Knee the day following the battle, on December 30, 1890.

Stranded 9th Cavalry

However, their supply wagon guarded by D Troop was located behind them was attacked by fifty Sioux warriors near Cheyenne Creek (about two miles from the Indian agency). One soldier was immediately killed. The wagon train protected itself by circling the wagons. Corporal William Wilson volunteered to take a message to the agency at Pine Ridge to get help after the Indian scouts refused to go. Wilson took off through the wagon circle with Sioux in pursuit and his troops covering him. Wilson reached the agency and spread the alarm. The 9th Cavalry within the agency came to the rescue of the stranded troopers and the Sioux dispersed.

"The Seventh Cavalry under the command of Colonel James W. Forsyth, was besieged in a canyon on White Clay Creek, with the Sioux commanding the heights on either side and threatening to cut off the retreat of the 7th Cavalry. The 7th Cavalry hunkered down and awaited rescue. Major Henry and the 9th halted at the mouth of the canyon. With the Hotchkiss firing away the Buffalo Soldiers surged forward shooting with deadly effect and emitting screams of elation at getting into battle. Confounded by the wave of Black soldiers surging toward them, the Sioux took to their heels. Without losing a man, the Buffalo Soldiers had recorded one of their most celebrated triumphs. **Newspapers across the nation proclaimed that Henry's troops had saved Forsyth from the same fate as Custer's fourteen years earlier.**

It was the last regiment to leave the Pine Ridge Reservation in the Winter of 1890–1891 following the massacre. (Source: Buffalo Soldiers and Officers of the Ninth Calvary 1867–1898, Charles L. Kenner, 1969, pages 125–128)

Major Henry lobbied the War Department tirelessly for a reward for the marvelous men of the 9th Cavalry. His efforts were rewarded as Troop K, 9th Cavalry and the 9th Cavalry Band arrived at Fort Myer on May 25, 1891, under the command of Major Henry.

This photograph was taken of the 9th Cavalry, "K" Company in Pine Ridge, South Dakota during the winter of 1890-91. Note the heavier coats, many Buffalo hide, and hats. Two men pictured here are Medal of Honor Winners- George Jordan, seated, and Henry Johnson, standing in rear. One of the Troopers pictured would be my great grandfather Alfred Pride

Buffalo Soldiers at Fort Myer, Virginia

FORT MYER—Fort Myer is the previous name used for a U.S. Army post next to Arlington National Cemetery in Arlington County, **Virginia**, and across the Potomac River from Washington, ... Published under the direction of the Secretary of War (1880–1891). Series 1 (Military Operations), Volume 36, Part 2, Chapter 48. (Source: Wikipedia).

No Buffalo Soldier unit had served east of the Mississippi River since Reconstruction, nor had one ever served near a significant center population. The first unit arrived at Fort Myer as part of a reward for their hard service during a brutal winter campaign against the Sioux Indians; known as the Pine Ridge Campaign. The Secretary of War announced the transfer and three remarkable distinctions occurred. Up to the outbreak of the war with Spain, it was the first black unit to serve at an east of the Mississippi; second, it was near a city of any size, and last, it was Fort Myer in the post-Reconstruction period. (Fowler 1970: pp. 133–134).

On May 22, 1891, Troop K of the 9th U.S. Cavalry left Fort Robinson, Nebraska by rail bound for Fort Myer and arrived on May 25, 1891. Upon arrival, the sixty-nine men and three officers received fifty-five serviceable horses and began training. Troop K performed routine garrison duties with other Fort Myer Cavalry units. Garrison duties consisted of drills, parades, practice, and still more practice, which differed from one season to another. If the weather proved inclement, there was a riding hall tucked away in one corner of the post in which the drills and shows could be performed.

Cavalry soldiers from Fort Myer were more than show soldiers; they were good saddle riders and complete masters of their horses. They practiced bareback on dead-level heats and jumped hurdles of varying heights that were designed to provide mastery and survival in the field. The soldiers were professionals who, on a moment's notice, could draw up in a line in front of the White House ready for either action or parade. On October 3, 1894, the 9th U.S. Horse Cavalry returned to Fort Robinson.

Internet Content 2020 – Public Domain
Fort Myer, VA. Again, I can only wonder, if one of them is Alfred Pride.

The 9th Cavalry served there until October 3, 1894, performing the duties of Presidential Parade Unit and ceremonial military burials at Arlington National Cemetery. The Henry Gate at Fort Myer is named after him.

Sergeant Pride was assigned to arguably the most decorated Company in any of the four Buffalo Soldier Regiments, Troop K, 9th Cavalry. He also served with the 10th Cavalry Regiment, Troop B and the 24th Infantry Regiment, Troop F at various times during his career. I don't know if his reason for his so many reenlistments, but the Army offered a steady income, housing, clothing, and food as well as an opportunity for some education. Few civilian jobs were offered at that time to the Black enlistees. For Black soldiers, the Army represented a career. Black soldiers took personal pride in their accomplishments. (Utley 1973: p. 26). Sergeant Pride was discharged from the Army in September 1893 with a rating of good. He retired to Washington, D.C., residing at 2600 I Street, N.W.

CHAPTER 7
1893–1910

(Retirement)

After they left the Army, the Black Regulars lived and died as quietly as they had before they enlisted. Most found unskilled or semi-skilled jobs. Most were the same jobs they could have obtained without the promises made. Records show that he worked as a hostler, laborer, bartender, and construction worker. I could find no record as to whether he drew a pension, although pensions helped some who could prove that they had been injured in the line of duty (I found no record he had been injured), but Congress did not grant "Indian wars" veterans a service pension until 1917. According to an article written by Erin Blakemore "Pensions for Veterans Were Once Viewed as a Government Handout" (November 10, 2018. History.com). There, once again, a reason that African Americans joined was to ensure a better quality of life but did not get the benefits of their long years of service.

In 1898, he married Matilda Hawkins whose mother Martha and Grandmother Malinda had been freed as slaves in Georgetown, D.C. on May 13, 1892, and lived, worked, and remained in Georgetown until his death. He died on August 2, 1910, of Apoplexy (stroke) and was buried at Arlington National Cemetery August 5, 1910, in Section 23, Site 16813. Wherever they lived and however poor they were, most veterans received decent funerals through the Office of the Federal Government, a fraternal order or their neighbor's charity. I have no knowledge of any other assistance, if any.

The 1800 act allowed widows to receive pensions if their husbands were disabled for any reason at the time of their death, not just due to injuries received in service. In 1901, a widow became eligible for a pension even if she had remarried, so long as she was again a widow. Congress was still averse to allowing a widow to receive money if she was still remarried. The rules on remarriage were also eased over time until the government no longer stopped any widow of an honorably discharged veteran from receiving aid in 1916. widows were not the only women to receive pensions. Union nurses began receiving them at the rate of twelve dollars a month in 1892. The Civil War pension system was color blind in that there was nothing in the application process that required applicants to be White. The federal pension system profoundly affected both the American political and economic systems in the decades after the war. (Source: Civil War Pensions, Kathleen Gorman). Widows became eligible in 1893. Three years later, pension payments began to those unable to economically care for themselves, again following the federal model. His widow Matilda Pride received twelve dollars per month pension as of March 4, 1917. When she died on March 20, 1928, her pension was thirty dollars per month. She is also buried in Arlington Cemetery. (Source: VA File WC 10020, Alfred Pride).

The Ft. Myer Military Community had a daytime series of events on September 18, 1937, to honor the 9th and 10th (Horse) Cavalry regiments. A wreath was laid at the grave of Sergeant Thomas Shaw (formerly of Company K), one of the six Buffalo Soldiers buried at Arlington National Cemetery who were so honored.

Alfred Pride's Grave Marker
Section 23, Site 16813

INTRODUCTION TO PART TWO

The doctrine of discovery was promulgated by European monarchies to legitimize the colonization of lands outside of Europe. Between the mid-fifteenth century and the mid-twentieth century, this idea allowed European entities to seize lands inhabited by indigenous peoples under the guise of discovering new land. In 1792, U.S. Secretary of State Thomas Jefferson claimed that this European Doctrine of Discovery was international law, which was applicable to the new U.S. Government as well (founded upon the model of European conquest: dispose of the disposable people). The doctrine and its legacy continue to influence American imperialism and treatment of indigenous and people of color.

The young American republic preserved this European doctrine. The U.S. supreme court formalized the Doctrine of Discovery in three famous cases of 1823, 1831, and 1832. Chief Justice John Marshall took for granted the obvious fact that America was the homeland of the Native Americans, "the rightful occupants of the soil." By the logic of "discovery," Native Americans had no rights because America was their homeland: "Their power to dispose of the soil at their own will to whomsoever they pleased was denied by the original fundamental principle that discovery gave exclusive title to those who made it." (Source: *The U.S. government should cede territory back to Native Americans*," Timothy Snider).

An Additional Adversary

Free Blacks, whether they could read and write, generally had no access to first-hand or second-hand unbiased information on this relationship, so they continued supporting the U.S. Government in its exercise of the "Manifest Destiny." Most Whites who had access often did not really care about the situation. It was business as usual in the name of "Manifest Destiny" Most [White] Americans viewed the Indians as incorrigible and non-reformable savages and convinced the African Americans of same. Those closest to the warring factions or who were threatened by it, naturally wanted government protection at any cost (Source: HistoryNet: Buffalo Soldiers in Black History). Because of their lack of knowledge as to the objective of the action, the Black soldiers sought to assist by engaging in government- and settler led wars meant to overtake the Southwest and Great Plains from Native Americans in return for their fully anticipated freedom.

You may ask the question "So why is the Doctrine of Discovery important today?" Because it has never been renounced. It remains the basis for Canadian Law and as such continues to impact Indigenous Peoples as well as people of color. This thinking has led to one of the problems facing America today, that of White supremacy. Because the Doctrine of Discovery has never been renounced, the White race has continued following the Manifest destiny, which was and still is for many, a widely held belief they are entitled to conquer and control North America

CHAPTER 8
Aftermath

Pawns

Why Did I Write this Chapter?

My original intent in writing this chapter was an aftermath after completing my research of my great grandfather's service in the Buffalo Soldiers with an intent to publish it as a historical record for future family generations. I became more interested in researching the Buffalo Soldiers in 1992, when General Colin Powell, the first Black Chairman of the Joint Chiefs of Staff returned to Fort Leavenworth to break ground for the Buffalo Soldiers memorial. On July 25, 1992, the bronze statue of a mounted trooper was unveiled among festive flags flying, bands playing and speeches that made them into a well-known widely familial cultural icon. This in addition to the movie "Glory," which was cast about the African Americans bravery in the Civil War led me to further research the bravery of the troopers in the Indian Wars.

After years of boasting with pride (no pun intended) and researching, I was now ready to publish about my newly found hero or patriot, Alfred Pride when the Black Lives Matter Movement began, and I became more interested in studying the racism that existed at that time with his and other units. It led me to trace their history from the post-slavery era and their formation to the end of his active service and life after retirement.

In writing this chapter, I based my assumptions on published information and known conditions existing at that time that may have been the influencing factors that led my great grandfather and others the decision to enlist in the Army, not realizing that many of the promises were not intended to be kept. I like many other African Americans had boasted with pride when hearing or reading about the exploits of the Buffalo Soldiers. While doing research on the ancestry of our maternal family in 2018, my niece discovered documents that my great grandfather had been a Buffalo Soldier. Upon finding out, he ran away from home in 1865 and put up his age to join, made me even more proud, so much so that I decided I would try to research his years of service, i.e., what made him join and what military campaigns he participated in. This was no small task because there was little information on the Black troopers, only their commanding officers and their units.

I assumed the reason he and other African American men joined the post-Civil War U.S. Army was for many reasons. One could be because he was a farmer, and the promise of land ownership could have been an overriding incentive. Although the war against slavery was over and the African Americans were supposedly granted full citizenship, they were far from free. Post-Civil War America offered few opportunities and little acceptance. The military provided thirteen dollars a month and a chance at building a new life in the aftermath of the war, not the least, the prospect of swapping the drudgery of sharecropping for an occupation that provided him with regular wages, the possibility of excitement, and a means of putting his anticipated newfound citizenship into action may have been his motivation. (Reviews in History: Men of Color to Arms. Elizabeth Leonard, 2011). He and many young African American men enlisted in the U.S. Army searching for the promised freedom and an opportunity to make a decent living. What they found was more discrimination and persecution. Ironically, these men were put into service helping the Army to oppress a race of people who had always known freedom. (Source: A Fight for Freedom by Dave Bieri). It was also known that those Native American nations had a legacy of racial division, segregation, and racial hierarchy that made them feel-as-a-whole. (America's 2nd Largest Indian Tribe Expels Blacks. NPR staff. September 20, 2011).

Inspired by the new thrust in the Black Lives Matters, I was led to concentrate my research on who were really the victims and/or who benefitted from the efforts of the Buffalo Soldiers despite the discrimination and horrible conditions they were forced to endure. After researching all, I decided that both the Native Americans and the African Americans, especially the Buffalo Soldiers were used by the U.S. Government, with the same objective as a pawn in a game of chess, i.e., to offer support in its effort to kill the King. In this case, the King being the various heads of the Indian Nations to take their land. If this were to be accomplished the European-American explorers would not have opposition in their quest to have dominion over the land and inhabitants of the North American continent. I have divided the aftermath of my book into two parts: The first part deals with the experiences of my Patriot Great Grandfather with the Buffalo Soldiers from his first enlistment in 1865 until his death in 1910. The second part deals with justifying my thinking that the Native Americans and the African Americans were deliberately used as pawns to satisfy the wishes of the U.S. Government and the European-American settlers in their quest to have dominion over the land and its inhabitants.

The Native Americans as Pawns

Who Gave the European Explorers the Power?

Since our country exists, we don't ask ourselves how or why. The legal foundation of the federal claim to dominion over territory is something called the Doctrine of Discovery, a notion that goes back five centuries. As European explorers sought new maritime passages and found new lands, popes granted European powers the authority to "invade, search out, capture, vanquish and subdue" the people they found. Indigenous peoples had no rights to land or to legal recognition of any kind. Only immigrants did. Portugal, Spain, France, and England claimed territory by planting a flag, a symbolic action known as "discovery." It made no difference whether the land in question was inhabited, as only Christians had conferred upon themselves the right to "discover" in this sense. By the logic of the papal bulls, and that of later charters to English explorers made by the English king or queen, indigenous peoples had no rights to land or to legal recognition of any kind. Only immigrants did.

The young American republic preserved this European doctrine. The U.S. supreme court formalized the Doctrine of Discovery in three famous cases of 1823, 1831, and 1832. Chief Justice John Marshall took for granted the obvious fact that America was the homeland of the Native Americans, "the rightful occupants of the soil." By the logic of "discovery," Native Americans had no rights because America was their homeland: "Their power to dispose of the soil at their own will to whomsoever they pleased was denied by the original fundamental principle that discovery gave exclusive title to those who made it." (Source: "The U.S. government should cede territory back to Native Americans," Timothy Snider).

An Additional Adversary

Free Blacks, whether they could read and write, generally had no access to first-hand or second-hand unbiased information on this relationship, so they continued supporting the U.S. Government in its exercise of the "Manifest Destiny." Most Whites who had access often did not really care about the situation. It was business as usual in the name of "Manifest Destiny." Most [White] Americans viewed the Indians as incorrigible and non-reformable savages and convinced the African Americans of same. Those closest to the warring factions or who were threatened by it, naturally wanted government protection at any cost (Source: HistoryNet: Buffalo Soldiers in Black History). Because of their lack of knowledge as to the objective of the action, the Black soldiers sought to assist by engaging in government- and settler-led wars meant to overtake the Southwest and Great Plains from Native Americans in return for their fully anticipated freedom.

MANIFEST DESTINY—A phrase coined in 1845, is the idea that the United States is destined—by God, its advocates believed—to expand the dominion and spread democracy and capitalism across the entire North American continent. The philosophy drove the nineteenth century U.S. territorial expansion and was used to justify the forced removal of Native Americans and other groups from their homes (Source: History.com editors).

Driven by their desires of fulfilling their belief in the Manifest Destiny and despite knowing that most of the Native American tribes sided with the British during the War of 1812 because they wanted to safeguard their tribal lands and with the hopes that a British victory would relieve the unrelenting pressure from the U.S. settlers, who wanted to push further into their land in Southern Canada and the lower Great Lakes and the South, the U.S. Government and the White settlers continued their quest to establish dominion over the West. The Native American tribes formed an alliance to aid the British, but the alliance started to weaken after the Battle of the Thames in Upper Canada considerably diminishing the power of the Native Americans east of the Mississippi to retain their homelands. A peace treaty compelled a tribe to surrender about twenty-three million acres of land (most of Southern Georgia and half of present-day Alabama) to the United States. Most of the Whites who had access did not care about the situation and continued driven by their belief that the United States was destined by God to expand their dominion over land and inhabitants.

Genocidal Intent

Slaves and the Black soldiers, who couldn't read or write, had no idea of the historical deprivations and the frequent genocidal intent of the U.S. Government toward Native Americans.

GENOCIDAL INTENT—The United Nations definition of genocide is as follows: "Any of the following acts, committed with intent to destroy, in whole or in part, a national, ethnical, racial or religious group, as such, killing, members of the group, causing serious bodily or mental harm to members of the group, deliberately inflicting on the group conditions of life calculated to bring about its physical destruction in whole or in part; imposing measures intended to prevent births within the group and forcibly transferring children of the group to another group." (Source: The U.S. against native Americans and the continued injustice today. Globetimes.com).

Given that the U.S. Government and American settlers waged wars, conducted mass killings, and destroyed Native Americans cultural conditions to prevent Indian tribes from surviving, it is clear, that the actions taken against Native Americans were genocidal. (Source: globetimes.com).

Indian Massacre

INDIAN MASSACRE—In the history of the European colonization of the Americas, an Indian massacre is any incident between European settlers and indigenous peoples wherein one group killed a significant number of the other group outside the confines of mutual combat in war.

"Indian massacre" is a phrase whose use and definition has evolved and expanded over time. The phrase was initially used by European colonists to describe attacks by indigenous Americans, which resulted in mass colonial casualties. While similar attacks by colonists on Indian villages were called "raids" or "battles," successful Indian attacks on White settlements or military posts were routinely termed "massacres." Knowing very little about the native inhabitants of the American frontier, the colonists were deeply fearful, and often, European Americans who had rarely—or never—seen a Native American read Indian atrocity stories in popular literature and newspapers. Emphasis was placed on the depredations of "murderous savages" in their information about Indians, and as the migrants headed further west, they frequently feared the Indians they would encounter. (Source: *"Conspiracy Theories in American History. An Encyclopedia;* Peter Knight, ABC-CLIO, 2003).

The phrase eventually became commonly used to also describe mass killings of American Indians. Killings described as "massacres" often had an element of indiscriminate targeting, barbarism, or genocidal intent. (Source: *Genocide and International Justice,* Rebecca Joyce Frey, InfoBase Publishing, 2009). A unknown historian once said, "Any discussion of genocide must, of course, eventually consider the so-called Indian Wars," the term commonly used for U.S. Army campaigns to subjugate Indian nations of the American West beginning in the 1860s.

Since the late twentieth century, it has become more common for scholars to refer to certain of these events as massacres, especially if there were large numbers of women and children as victims. This includes the Colorado territorial militia's slaughter of Cheyenne at Sand Creek (1864), and the U.S. Army's slaughter of Shoshone at Bear River (1863), Blackfeet on the Marias River (1870) and Lakota at Wounded Knee (1890). Some scholars have begun referring to these events as "genocidal massacres," defined as the annihilation of a portion of a larger group, sometimes to provide a lesson to the larger group. (Source: Genocide and International Justice: Rebecca Joyce Frey; InfoBase Publishing, 2009).

Cultural Assimilation

The policy of assimilation was an attempt to destroy traditional Indian cultural identities. Many historians have argued that the U.S. Government believed that if American Indians did not adopt European-American culture, they would become extinct as a people. This paternalistic attitude influenced interactions between American Indian nations and the U.S. Government throughout the first half of the 1800s, and its efforts continue to be felt today. (Source: Federal Acts and Assimilation Policies. Usdakotawar.org).

ASSIMILATION – The process whereby individuals or groups of differing ethnic heritage are absorbed into the dominant culture of a society. (Source: Britannica.com).

During the late nineteenth century, when most Native Americans were confined to reservations, the federal government engaged in a "cultural assimilation" campaign by forcing thousands of Native American children to attend boarding schools. Between 1880 and 1902, some 100,000 Native Americans were forced to attend these schools, forbidden to speak Native languages, made to renounce Native beliefs, and forced to abandon their Native American identities, including their names. Parents who resisted their children's removal to boarding schools were imprisoned and had their children forcibly taken from them. The Bureau of Indian Affairs also threatened the parents with imprisonment in an attempt, to force them to adopt farming practices that were inconsistent with their cultural values. (Source: *Cultural genocide and the Native American children.* eji.org).

While the concerted effort to assimilate Native Americans into American culture was abandoned officially, integration of Native American tribes and individuals continue to the present day. Often Native Americans are perceived as having been assimilated. However, some Native Americans feel a particular sense of being from another society or do not belong in a primarily "White" European majority society despite efforts to socially integrate them. (Source: *Cultural Assimilation.* En.m.wikipedia.org).

Today's Viewpoint (The Missing Apology)

Two centuries later we are just seeing some of those past atrocities being addressed. Relatives of a Yuchi Indian tribe member who was marched across the country on the Trail of Tears is pushing for the United States to acknowledge the official apology it has already made to Native American peoples, which was buried in a defense-spending bill and signed into law in 2010 (Source: Washington Post article by Emily McFarlan Miller, July 30, 2021). Negriel Bigpond who is Yuchi, and Sam Brownback, the former governor and U.S. Ambassador have launched a movement to raise awareness of the apology and asked President Biden to formally recognize it in a ceremony at the White House Rose Garden. "I just felt it was time that the Native people receive an apology from this nation said Brownback." I also think it is past time that an official public apology delivered by the President of the United States is in order, to right the unfilled promises to the Buffalo Soldiers.

In the Department of Defense Appropriations Act of 2010, Congress "recognized that there had been years of official depredation, ill-conceived policies and the breaking of covenants by the Federal Government regarding Indian tribes," but to date I do not know of any resolutions passed by Congress, apologizing to the Buffalo Soldiers, who in my opinion were used by the government against the Native Americans in the name of the "Manifest Destiny" idea, with no real intent to fulfill its promises of full citizenship to them or the African American people.

Today's Native American

Today, Native American communities are diverse and complex, and can be found across the United States, in cities and rural areas, on tribal land or far away. Tribal governments' relationships with federal, state, and local governments remain complex, and issues about land sovereignty and use are debated in legislatures and contested in the courts.

Many of the rights secured by Native Americans were won through the efforts of activist groups in the twentieth century, such as the American Indian Movement. Today, new generations of activists and tribal leaders continue to fight to improve the life and culture of Native American communities and to force the government to honor many of the treaties.

From California to Maine, land is being given back to Native American tribes who are committing to managing it for conservation or environmental purposes. Are they again being used as pawns because of their knowing how to support wildlife, to the use of prescribed fires, to protect their ancestral grounds or being used to recapture land and wildlife loss to mismanagement by the White man?

Along with the enslavement of Black Americans, this forced land dispossession is one of the country's most significant transgressions. Many of the biggest challenges facing Native American communities today, from rampart poverty to lower social and economic mobility to health issues cast in high relief by the pandemic, can be traced to the attempted extermination and then assimilation of Native Americans [and African Americans] through American land policy (Source: The Hill.com).

Is the campaign to return Indian land as part of the racial justice movement that is sweeping the globe or another "Bait and Switch" after its revitalization?

It is my hope that this new movement is not another "Field Order 15" that will be reversed once the tribe has revitalized the land. I feel it is heavenly driven by the fact that so much land and property are being lost through wildfires because of mismanagement or lack of know how. The Esselen Tribe of California, which had inhabited the Big Sur region for thousands of years, was stripped of its culture and lands by the Spanish, who built missions in the region. The Western Rivers Conservancy, with funding from the California Natural Resources Agency, arranged the purchase of a 1,199-acre ranch with redwood forest and a crystalline stream, the Little Sur, where steelhead spawn, to protect it and planned to donate it to the U.S. Forest Service. Locals objected, and so last year, they instead transferred the property, valued at $4.5 million, to the Esselen – 250 years after it was taken. The tribe says it will protect natural values, including spawning steelhead, the California spotted owl, the endangered California condor and habitat that connects the ocean to the Santa Lucia Mountains, as well as use the land for traditional ceremonies and plant gathering.

In many cases, tribes are buying land that is important to them. In Northern California, the Yurok Tribe, the largest tribe in California, owns forty-four miles of land along the Klamath River. They have been piecing back their aboriginal lands, with the help of land conservation groups such as the Trust for Public Land and Western Rivers Conservancy, to protect the habitat of their primary food source, salmon, and to assure access to ceremonial grounds and other cultural landscapes. The Yurok have purchased more than 80,000 acres to add to their holdings, including 50,000 acres that had been owned by a timber company and surround four salmon spawning streams that the tribe now plans to restore. (Source: *How Returning Lands to Native Americans is Helping Protect Nature.* E360.yale.edu).

Proposed Reparation

Much of the campaign to return Indian land or at least allow co-management is part of the racial justice movement that is sweeping the globe. In the American Indian community, it's called Landback—and some in that movement see a more radical form of reconciliation.

In a recent article in the *Atlantic*, David Treuer, a Native American, citing the litany of forced removal and broken treaties that enabled the creation of U.S. national parks, advocated for giving a consortium of Native American tribes the ownership and management responsibility—with binding covenants to protect natural values—for all eighty-five million acres of the national park system, as reparations in kind for land that was stolen from them. "The total acreage would not quite make up for the General Allotment Act, which robbed us of 90 million acres, but it would ensure that we have unfettered access to our tribal homelands," he wrote. "And it would restore dignity that was rightfully ours. To be entrusted with the stewardship of America's most precious landscape would be a deeply meaningful form of restitution." Still, there are some concerns about possible downsides to tribal management. Will tribes allow hunting in places where it hasn't been allowed because of tradition? Or will a change in tribal administrations alter policies toward ecologically important lands that no longer favor protection?

Is it Deja Vu Over Again?

All over California to Maine, land is being given back to Native American tribes who are committing to managing it for conservation or environmental purposes. Are they again being used as pawns because of their knowing how to support wildlife, to the use of prescribed fires, to protect their ancestral grounds or being used to recapture land and wildlife loss to mismanagement [by the White man]?

Indian Givers (no pun intended)

In the early years of contact, Europeans viewed gifts from generous Native Americans as gifts, while the Indians saw this as an exchange for which they expected something in return [compare this thinking with the Buffalo Soldiers reason for volunteering]. Seen in terms of original territory of the Flathead tribes. Seen in terms of original territory of the Flathead tribes, the proposal to transfer the land to the Indians seem more like a give-back, rather than a give-away as claim by those in opposition. In any case, the land will still be under the trusteeship of the Bureau of Indian Affairs. [Sounds like another Field Order 15—I am giving you back your land, but you don't own it].

FLATHEAD RESERVATION—The Flathead Reservation located in western Montana on the Flathead River is home to the Bitterroot Salish, Kootenai, and Pend d'Oreilles tribes – also known as the Confederated Salish and Kootenai Tribes of the Flathead Nation. The reservation was created through the July 16, 1855, Treaty of Hellgate. (Source: Wikipedia).

Nothing has Changed

At the outset the Europeans and settlers viewed the Indians as incorrigible and nonreformable savages, and further believed that unless culturally assimilated to European-American culture, they would become extinct as a people. Evidently, vestiges of this thinking still exist today, as evidenced by government wanting to keep control of the land on the Indian reservations. A case in point. The Flathead Indian tribes ceded over twenty million acres of their land to the federal government, which left them with a 1.3-million-acre reservation. In 2016, a lawsuit was filed to stop the give-back, because among other things, it was thought the Indians would not know how to manage the bison as well as the bureaucrats, although under the government, the Bison Range had been severely neglected. Although the tribes had shown they were fully capable and demonstrated with the timber management and cultural sites management their capability, there was still opposition, despite these successes, e.g. better species and distribution of trees, making them less prone to wildfires, better wildlife habitat and better water quality. Because of their management, they have earned two dollars for every one dollar spent compared to the U.S. Forest Service simply breaking even. Opposing tribal land management harkens back to the Burke Act of 1906 that locked Indian land into the Trusteeship of the federal government until and unless the government ordains Indians to be "competent and capable." Transferring federal lands back to Native Americans would be a good first step toward expunging that racist notion from our national policies. (Source: *Terry Anderson, Opinion Contributor*. thehill.com).

Lasting Effects

Along with the enslavement of Black Americans, this forced land dispossession is one of the country's most significant transgressions. Many of the biggest challenges facing native communities today, from rampant poverty to lower social and economic mobility to health issues cast in high relief by the pandemic, can be traced to the attempted extermination and then assimilation of Native Americans [and African Americans] through American land policy (Source: The Hill.com).

Troopers and Other Blacks as Pawns
Unwanted from the Beginning

The hostility against the Black troopers was there not only from the Native Americans but also from the White majority from their initial organization and even some in the North. Despite their reluctance to allow Blacks to join the military at first, the escalating number of former slaves (contrabands), the declining number of white volunteers and the pressing needs of the Union Army pushed the government to reconsider the ban. After the Emancipation, Black recruitment was pursued in earnest. Recruitment was slow until Frederick Douglass and other Black leaders encouraged Black men to become soldiers to ensure eventual full citizenship [which still has not been realized]. Although allowed to join, the intent was to relegate them to noncombat support roles, i.e., carpenters, Chaplains, cooks, guards, laborers, nurses, scouts, spies, steamboat pilots, surgeons, and teamsters to contribute to the war cause (Source: Black soldiers in the U.S. Military during the Civil War. Archives.gov). Many of the [White] officers refused to command Black regiments. In addition, Blacks could only serve west of the Mississippi

River, because many Whites did not want to see armed Black soldiers in or near their communities. They viewed their main task as helping to control the Native Americans of the Plains, capture cattle rustlers and thieves, and protect settlers, stagecoaches, wagon trains, and railroad crews along the Western front, not them. They were also afraid if Black troops were armed, they would turn on them in retaliation for their past atrocities. With the Black troopers being utilized in the westward expansion, it freed up the [White] troopers in the East to assist in the turbulent era following the Civil War and its efforts to reintegrate Southern states from the Confederacy and the nearly four million newly freed people into the United States.

As soon as these soldiers enlisted with their promise of full citizenship and possibly land and with minimal training, they were relocated into their hostile environments, where they were engaged in life and death struggles. They were under fire. Friends were killed and their oath to keep the peace, put to the test by Indians, settlers, and those outside the law. Meanwhile, while guarding railroads and telegraph lines, stagecoaches, arms shipments, towns, homesteads, Whites, and Indians, they never knew when they would be ambushed by foes or the very townspeople they were protecting! Not infrequently, just by entering a town or saloon, shoot-outs occurred. There was also the occasional sniper, waiting for a kill. Those White settlers that murdered Black troopers were never punished for their crimes, even when there were witnesses. The troopers always responded with a deadly intent of their own. When investigated by the military, those troopers found guilty were punished accordingly, but not always justly. This closely parallels today's White policemen and African American males' occurrences that's frequently happening.

While Black soldiers were fighting Native Americans in the West, African American men, women, and children were still being lynched, segregated, persecuted in the East, and having laws passed that would deter, if not stop, them from gaining full citizenship. In the West, the Buffalo Soldiers were often viewed with hostility, even by the people of the frontier settlements that their regiments were protecting. This is evident in the treatment of the African American and Native Americans today. This hostility often erupts in violence. Efforts at protecting settlements in hostile territory often went unrewarded and unappreciated. You can relate that to current events where often the aggressors are not persecuted.

Promise of Land

Despite the many barriers and challenges faced by those who sought to own land, African Americans saw land ownership as a pathway to independence, and a confirmation of their freedom. The Civil War period brought many legislative enactments that ostensibly provided recently enslaved African Americans with opportunities for the acquisition of real property. These efforts served as the primary basis for the belief that African Americans would receive "forty acres and a mule" at the conclusion of the Civil War. Opponents to African American's quest for land ownership were vehement in their efforts. (Source: In the Beginning: Origins of African American Real Property Ownership in the United States by Roy W. Copeland. *Journal of Black Studies*. Vol. 44, No. 6 [September 2013]. pp. 646-664).

The "Big" Lie

When slavery was abolished in 1865, Black Americans started to demand American land. An incentive for Black men to join the Army was the expectation of one day owning their own land. One of the responses offered to their demand was Field Order 15 issued through what is famously referred to as the Savannah Colloquy. The order gave roughly 400,000 acres of land that lay on the coastline of Georgia and South Carolina to freed slaves. The confiscated land from previous slave owners, planters, and/or plantation owners extended about thirty miles inland from the Atlantic Ocean and stretching from Charleston, South Carolina 245 miles south to Jacksonville, Florida. In addition, the mules, although not a part of the order, that had been used in the war and were now idle were to be offered to these Black Americans for use in farming.

> **SPECIAL FIELD ORDER 15**—The order encouraged the enlistment of "young and able-bodied negroes" in the service of the United States and guaranteed anyone enlisting the right to "locate his family in any one of the settlements at pleasure." Finally, the order provided that "no white person whatever, unless military officers and soldiers detailed for duty, will be permitted to reside; and the sole and exclusive management of affairs will be left to the freed people themselves, subject only to the United States military authority and the acts of Congress." (Source: Wikipedia).

Two weeks later, William Henry Trescot, who was in Washington to lobby on behalf of those South Carolinians whose land had been confiscated, met with Sherman and other officers to discuss the genesis of Special Field Order No. 15.

Bait and Switch

Sherman told the group that his intention was to offer a temporary solution. In a follow-up letter to the president, he wrote, "I knew of course we could not convey title and merely provided possessory titles, to be good as long as War and our Military Power lasted. I merely aimed to make provision for the Negroes who were absolutely dependent upon us, leaving the value of their possession to be determined by after events or legislation." As one historian has argued, "What the general has managed in No. 15 was a strategist version of bait and switch."

In the summer of 1865 after the assassination of President Lincoln, President Andrew Jackson reversed the order of General William T. Sherman and ordered all lands under federal control to be returned to previous owners. The freedmen and women [many of whom could have been Black troopers' families] who received the land offer as an incentive for their family member to join were informed they could either sign labor contracts with the planters or be evicted from the land they occupied by the Army troops. This left most Black people living in rural areas of the South forced to work as laborers on White-owned farms and plantations or as sharecroppers with the White owners. A promised reparation that never came to fruition. With that bitter legacy in mind "The 40 Acres and a Mule Project" seeks to foster Black equity by reclaiming land that was promised and then taken back.

> **40 Acres & A Mule Project**—A project to buy forty acres of land to be Black owned with its goal to (1) use the land to guarantee farm to table resources for the food industry; (2) serve to provide an outlet for Black foodways; and (3) establish a safe-haven to secure the legacy of Black foodways.

The Driving Force

The Black soldiers, who fought in the Indian Wars, fought their opponents as they have done throughout the country's military history. They fought to win and to give their lives, if necessary, for their personal beliefs. They wanted to gain the respect and equality they never saw as slaves and rarely received as freedmen. One of the driving forces was the anticipated gain of land, which was viewed as being fully freed and had been advanced as an incentive for their joining. So, they continued enlisting as soldiers (where they earned better than average pay) to enable them, one day to purchase their own land. They were sadly mistaken in thinking they would gain these components of freedom, in a county built in part by their enslavement and which held deep racial and cultural practices.

The Big "Gotcha"

Vaughnette Goode-Walker, a writer who leads tours focused on Savannah, Georgia's Black past calls it one of the biggest "gotcha's" in American history.

"Here, take this land – but we can't really give it to you because it doesn't belong to us; it belongs to the Confederate when they come back home."

The Real Victims

The National Museum of African History and Culture states that "Black soldiers were using service as a strategy to obtain their equal rights as citizens." They fought in all the major Indian conflicts, even against some tribes who had Black members (free and enslaved), e.g., Cherokee, Seminole and Creek. They fought in the 1874-75 Red River War against several different tribes and the final campaigns against the Apaches in the following decade. In Elizabeth Leonard's book *Men of Color* (2011), she stated that both American Indians and Native Americans were victims (not always passive ones, it must be stressed) of White racism. They too were used as pawns in the name of the "Manifest Destiny" (the belief held by many White citizens of the United States that their system is best and the idea that all humans would like to or need to become Americans).

While enduring unimaginable hardships and racial prejudice, the Black troopers proved to be competent soldiers and invaluable to the U.S. Army. My great grandfather as a member of one of these African American regiments spent over twenty-five years engaged in fighting Native Americans, mapping unexplored lands, and opening the West for settlement. Unfortunately, he and his fellow Black troopers received little recognition for their service on the frontier, although their White commanding officers and their units were often cited for their victories. While over 400 veterans of the Indian Wars received Congressional Medals of Honor, only eighteen African American enlisted men received the award despite being in the forefront of the fighting throughout the quarter century long conflict. (Source: A fight for Freedom by Dave Bieri).

Further Disrespect

Although State and federal leaders from President Lincoln down had promised to care for "those who have borne the burden, his widows and orphans," they had little knowledge of how to accomplish this task. There was also little political pressure to see that the promises were kept. (Source: *"Sons of Union Veterans of the Civil War"* – National Headquarters). As a result, many Buffalo Soldiers who toiled through the Indian Wars were denied pensions [not known about my great grandfather] unless they could prove they were injured in the line of duty or had fought in an Indian War. Upon return home, nothing much had changed, and they had to compete with non-veterans for the low-paying jobs.

At retirement pensions helped some who could prove that they had been injured in the line of duty, but Congress did not grant "Indian wars" veterans a service pension until 1917. (This was of no benefit to my great grandfather who died in 1910). His widow started receiving a pension on March 4, 1917 (seven years after his death) for twelve dollars per month. When she died in 1928 it has risen to thirty dollars per month.

New Hope Back Home

In 1866, Congress passed the Southern Homestead Act. This Act was meant to avail land in states such as Alabama, Arkansas, Florida, Louisiana, Texas, and Mississippi to acquisition by the people, which included the Black population. At the core of Act was the endeavor to give Black Americans the chance to buy land in these states, of which some Black Americans took advantage. Though Black Americans' right to land was improving, their political and social rights, among others, were declining at a worrying pace, especially in the South.

The Federation of Southern Cooperatives was created in 1867 and was intended to offer financial assistance to Black farmers to assist in their quest to acquire land and to improve their agricultural practices. A second Morill Act was passed in 1890 and gave Blacks grants to colleges to learn arts and agricultural courses. In line with this, Black Americans formed the first cooperative union in Arkansas and the United States in order to fight for and protect their rights.

The rest of these eras is characterized by the Jim Crow policies that had been legalized by the Supreme Court under the *Plessy v. Ferguson* 1896 decision that allowed "separate but equal" treatment of Whites and Blacks.

For a period after the Civil War, Black ownership of land increased and was primarily used for farming. At one point, Blacks had gained ownership over about fifteen million acres, which meant that they were also in control of 14 percent of the farms located in the United States (that is 925,000 farms owned by Black people).

Start of the Decline

By 1910, records showed that more Black Americans owned land than ever before in the history of the United States. Over fourteen million acres of land were owned by approximately 210,000 Black persons, leading some historians to refer to this period as the height of Black land ownership. Since then, however, Black land ownership has been on a steady decline.

In 2002, a USDA Report showed that Black people owned less than 1 percent of the rural land in the United States and the total value of all that land together is only fourteen billion dollars, out of a total land value of more than 1.2 trillion dollars, while the total land that White people owned 96 percent of rural land, bringing their land's joint worth to just over one trillion dollars.

Black American farmers are more likely to rent rather than own the land on which they live, which in turn made them less likely to be able to afford to buy land later.

In the year 2010, President Barack Obama authorized the payment of 1.25 billion dollars from the USDA to Black American farmers as a settlement in *Pigford* v. *Glickman*. Even after the Pigford settlement Black land loss remained prevalent. The awarding has been put on hold by the courts as being unfair to the white farmers.

Black Land Loss Impact on the Present

Land ownership in minority communities is particularly important as it is often one of the few (and largest) forms of wealth. During slavery, Black people were denied ownership of themselves let alone land and after slavery ended, laws were set in place to ensure that this remained the same. Land ownership is one of the easier ways to establish wealth, but Black people were denied this option for so long that now it is one of the only forms of wealth they have. (Source: Black Land Loss in the U.S. Wikipedia).

Why Are They Not Being Challenged to Contribute Some Land Back?

This also raises the question "was it the fact that land is power, land is wealth and more importantly land is about race and class the reason it was not one of the categories that America's fifty biggest companies did not commit any of their financial contributions to reparation for stolen land from Black farmers?" Although some of the richest private investors, have contributed to some of the categories, they too have not contributed too or offered any of their vast accumulations of land as reparation, e.g., it has been reported that Bill Gates is the biggest private owner of farmland in the United States. His 242,000 acres is twice the acreage of the Lower Brule Sioux tribe. (Source: Nick Estes); Ted Turner owns two million acres and has the world's largest privately owned buffalo herd preserved today on nearly 200,000 acres of Turner's ranch land within the boundaries of the 1868 Fort Laramie Treaty Territory in what is now the State of Montana, land that was once guaranteed by the U.S. Government to be a permanent home for Lakota people. The Teachers Insurance and Annuity Association (TIAA) owns 233,000 acres of farmland spread across twelve states including CA, WA, FL, and WI. In the Mississippi Delta and nearby fertile crescent of Arkansas, it holds more than 120,000 acres along a strip of counties along the Mississippi River. In just a few years, a single company has accumulated a portfolio in the Delta almost equal to the remaining holdings of African Americans who have lived on and shaped the land for centuries. (Source: theatlantic.com). In just a few years, a single company has accumulated a portfolio in the Delta almost equal to the remaining holdings of the African Americans who have lived on and shaped this land for centuries. Although, TIAA played no part in the loss and legally sanctioned theft of the land, the land was wrested first from the Native Americans by force. It was then cleared, watered, and made productive for intensive agriculture by the labor of enslaved Africans, who after Emancipation would come to own a portion of it. Later through a variety of means—sometimes legal, often coercive, in many cases legal and coercive, occasionally violent—farmland owned by Black people came into the hands of White people. This is also an indicator that the thinking of the "Manifest Destiny" is still-alive, and the Buffalo Soldiers were a part of that chess game and used to fulfill the objective of having dominion of the land and its inhabitants and did not have any of the land taken from the Indians deeded for their use. (Source: Blackland Loss in the U.S. Wikipedia. [en.m.Wikipedia.org.]).

Self-confession—In my research of this topic, I read a statement that that stated "If you're one of the millions of people who have a retirement account with the Teachers Insurance Annuity Association, for instance, you might even own a little bit yourself. I am guilty of belonging."

New Thoughts

I now found myself rethinking as to whether I was proud of the accomplishments of the Buffalo Soldiers from a humanistic viewpoint. It comes at a time of racial reckoning across the country, and there is an awakening that it is time to recognize and right wrongs. Yes, I was still proud of my great grandfather's service record and his military achievements but was I proud of the role the Black soldiers had been assigned to carry out. to benefit the so called "Manifest Destiny?" At the heart of which was the pervasive belief in American cultural and racial superiority. Expanding the boundaries of the United States was in many ways a cultural war as well. The desire of the southerners to find more lands suitable for cotton cultivation that would eventually spread slowly to these regions. It was further driven by its belief that it was God's will that Americans [White men] spread out over the entire continent and ordained them to control and populate the country as they see fit.

Chances for a Reconciliation of Thought

As talks of reparation which have been a confrontational topic for most Americans and the asking for apologies grew, it made me wonder who or if there is an organized body fighting the cause of the Buffalo Soldiers. Yes, I know there was a statue dedicated at Fort Leavenworth because of the efforts of General Colin Powell, but where was the demand for an official public apology as the American Indians is now seeking from the U.S. Government?

Reparation—The making of amends for a wrong one has done, by paying money to or otherwise helping those who have been wronged (Source: Wikipedia).

What Are and What Was the Views of the American Indian

Realizing where there are numbers, there is strength led me to think whether there would become a joining of forces in seeking reparations? What are the views of the Native American about the Buffalo Soldiers? It made me question if the Buffalo Soldiers were viewed in a positive light by the Native Americans or in the same negative light as Confederate soldiers are viewed in the eyes of the African American for helping take their land and freedom. In my research, I read an article on "Myths of the Buffalo Soldiers" in Black Valor, by Frank N. Schubert, Buffalo Soldiers, and the Medal of Honor, 1870–1898, that the name "Buffalo Soldiers" as a sign of respect by Indian warriors has not gone unchallenged. The most serious objection has come from Contemporary Native American leaders who were angered over the publicity attending the issuance of a buffalo soldier postage stamp in 1994 and resented the suggestion that there was some special bond between the soldiers and their warrior ancestors. The first salvo of dissent came from Vernon Bellecourt of the American Indian Movement. Writing in the *Indian Country Today*, a reliable forum for objections to glorification of Buffalo Soldiers, Bellecourt denied that the name reflected any "endearment or respect." As far as he was concerned, Plains Indians only applied the term Buffalo Soldiers to "these marauding murderous cavalry units" because of "their dark skin and texture of their hair." In fact, Black soldiers never seemed to use "Buffalo Soldiers" in their letters to Black newspapers, in court-martial testimony or in pension applications. Among them, "buffalo" was an insult. . . although, many Black Regulars had great racial as well as professional pride, they did not express it by a nickname. "Buffalo Soldiers" seem to have been a term that appealed to outsiders, but insiders did not use. (Source: Facts and information about the African American Cavalry Regiment known as Buffalo Soldiers in Black History. HistoryNet).

As historian William Gwaltney, a descendant of Buffalo Soldiers, said, "Buffalo Soldiers fought for recognition as citizens in a racist country and . . . American Indian people fought to hold on to their land, and their lives." These were not comparable, harmonious goals that could provide the basis for interracial harmony. The only obstacles the Buffalo Soldiers could not overcome were those of prejudice and discrimination, which still exist today.

It is Public or Formal Apology Time

I also think it is past time that an official public apology delivered by the President of the United States is in order, to right the unfilled promises to the Buffalo Soldiers. But to date, I do not know of any resolutions passed by Congress, apologizing to the Buffalo Soldiers, who in my opinion were used by the government against the Native Americans in the name of the "Manifest Destiny" idea, with no intent to fulfill its promises of full citizenship to them or the African American people. The African Americans and/or their families were victims of broken proclamations (Emancipation), forced removal from land (Field Order 15), and other mistreatments as the Troopers fought to further the westward movement. Citing Brownback, "we're in a season of reconciliation. This is a time where we're wrestling with these sins of the nation – whether it was toward the First Nation, whether it was slavery [or the utilization of fulfilling the idea of the Manifest Destiny] – where we're wrestling with these problems now and their consequences. It's time to deal with it." Bigpond also stated, "I believe it would help – not so much that we would get granted great finances and buy the land or give the land back or anything like that. It was a spiritual thing." Bigpond said, "An apology would be good medicine to heal people and heal the land." That is why I am adamant in my belief that my great grandfather and the Buffalo Soldiers who fought in the Indian Wars are owed an official apology for being used to help settle the West, with no follow-up or effort to fulfill the promises of full citizenship, forty acres of land, or apologies for their mistreatment.

For the land stolen from the African Americans, a 1.9 trillion Covid relief package approved five billion dollars (a mere pittance) in relief for Black farmers, but that has been blocked by a Judge that it discriminates against white farmers. According to the Census of Agriculture, 100 years ago, in 1920, there were about 13,000 Black farm operators in our state. Today, that number sits at about 2,000. That is a 74 percent decrease. Over the past 100 years, Black farmers in the United States have lost more than twelve million acres of farmland. If I was a betting man, I would wager a bet that most research will show that the land was lost through an action of the government, e.g., eminent domain, wills (obstacles to filing), foreclosures, housing they can't afford, or other amenities for the benefit of the majority. The manifest destiny is still in existence and their belief in American cultural and racial superiority is still a driving factor.

Conclusion

My great grandfather and his Buffalo Soldiers could in any ways you look at it, after researching his service record, be called Patriots according to its definition.

PATRIOT—a person who vigorously supports their country and is prepared to defend it against enemies or detractors (Source: Definitions from Oxford Languages).

This viewpoint was shared by me and others. Using the game of chess and its strategies as an evaluation tool of the Buffalo Soldiers service and their reward, I have come to the following conclusion. African American soldiers and the Native Americans were used as pawns to enable the U.S. Government to carry out "The Manifest Destiny" (to spread democracy and capitalism across the entire North American continent). The U.S. Government used both the Native Americans and the African Americans in the same role as a pawn in a chess game to manipulate it so the government could confiscate their land to accomplish the objectives of the Manifest Destiny. Does the idea of Manifest Destiny still exist today? In a way, it still happens in the United States. Although it may not be exactly like the one, we learned about in history class. It is still a very similar concept that some people today would even call it Manifest Destiny. An example of it is the belief held by many citizens of the United States that their system is the best and the idea that all humans would like to become Americans as the idea coined in 1845 that the United States is destined—by God, its advocates believe—to expand its dominion and spread democracy and capitalism across the North American continent (Essay by Ben Jones, May 8, 2021, Myorganizing.org). Up until today, the discrimination and oppression against ethnic minorities goes on in the United States. Racial discrimination is systemic in American society. Native Americans, African Americans, and other minorities are still in dire straits (Source: The U.S. Genocide against Native Americans and the continued injustice today. Globetimes.com).

The chess game is still being played today, as the government is still exercising or taking another approach to its belief that they are operating under God's destiny. Both groups (Native American and African Americans) are still fighting to control the land and other amenities promised to them by the varies treaties and policies. The Native Americans are still being used by offering them back land that was taken from them without the realization that it is not an apology, but for environmental purposes, the African Americans are having their land taken from them through fraud, eminent domain, and foreclosure, making their heroic acts in vain, as they still didn't receive the freedoms they were promised in return for their service. For many Black Americans, echoing past wrongs, the thousand acres of land given to, and the thousands taken back from the descendants of enslaved African Americans is an enduring legacy. So, any effort to return land to Black farmers represents a very important effort at restorative justice. Because of their heroism, some Buffalo Soldiers were able to get better jobs, own property, or gain access to higher education, and at the same time, some returning Buffalo Soldiers were lynched. African Americans realized that the sacrifices made by them for their service have not yet made us equal citizens. To me they were manipulated by the government who used them as pawns to settle the West with their labor, but the government had no intention to grant them with the full freedom, enjoyed by the white man.

I do not hold my great grandfather personally accountable for his involvement, for he like others was merely following the instructions of the ones who personally benefitted by the so-called "Manifest Destiny" (was it "the first Big Lie") in exchange for an anticipated better quality of life. It was a lack of knowledge of why this action was being undertaken that led to this "breach?"

If it is warranted, I apologize for my great grandfather whose actions at that time were the accepted norm and provided him an upgrade to the average living condition, but in the end did not reward him with the freedoms he anticipated. This in no way diminishes the pride I have of my great grandfather, who is my hero, or the Buffalo Soldiers accomplishments. Yes, they may have been used as pawns in the governments grand scheme of things, but they changed the negative perceptions held by the white man of their bravery, commitment, and abilities.

HERO—a person of distinguished courage or ability, admired for his or her brave deeds and noble qualities.

EXHIBITS

(Exhibit 1)

Transcript of Alfred Pride's First Court Martial

Convened on June 28, 1973

Lieutenant John Bigelow found the following letter in his room:

Thursday, December 20, 1877 ... I found a letter in my room, written for Private Alfred Pride to Gen'l Ord:

Sir,

I wish to inform the Gen'l Comd'g of the unjust manner in which I was treated. My company was paid ... (on) Decb'r 13th 1877. Being absent on detached service I was not paid ... I presented myself to (the Paymaster) at 3 P.M. yesterday but he refused to pay me saying his safe was locked up. I have been nearly six months without pay and need the money, and request (it)... be sent to me in a check.

Court Martial of Private Alfred Pride, Company B, 10th Cavalry/ Fort Sill, Indian Territory
Convened on June 28, 1873 at 10 o'clock A.M.
Charge: "Neglect of duty, to the prejudice of good order and military discipline"
Specification: "That Private Alfred Pride, Co. B, 10th Cavalry, having been duly placed as sentinel in charge of George Davis, Private of Co. I, 10th Cavalry, a general prisoner awaiting trial by general court martial for desertion, did allow said Davis to escape from him, said prisoner Davis being at the time shackled. This at Fort Gibson, I.T. on the 24th of March 1873
To which charge and specification the accused pleaded "Not Guilty"
Finding: The court, having maturely considered the evidence presented, finds the accused not guilty of the specification and not guilty of the charge, And the court does therefore acquit him

Detail for Court: Captain G.K. Sanderson, 11th Infantry; Captain C.F. Robe, 25th Infantry; 1st Lieutenant R.G. Smither, 10th Cavalry; 1st Lieutenant S. Pepoon, 10th Cavalry; Second Lieutenant L.A. Matile, 11th Infantry; Second Lieutenant L. H. Orleman, 10th Cavalry. Judge Advocate: First Lieutenant L.H. Orleman, Adjutant 10th Cavalry

9:00A.M., Ft. Sill, I.T. July 9, 1873 (??)
The Court then proceeded to the trial of Alfred Pride, Private of Co. B, 10th Cavalry, who being called before the Court and having heard the order appointing its need, was asked if he had any objection to any member present, named in the order, to which he replied in the affirmative, and objected to 2nd Lieutenant L. H. Orleman, 10th Cavalry, for the reason that he believes he is prejudiced against him. The prisoner had no evidence to offer to substantiate the fact, except for his own statement as to his belief.

Lt. L. H. Orleman, the challenged member, being then duly sworn according to the law, made the following statement: I am not a witness in the case, but being Officer of the Day at the time the affair with which the prisoner is charged occurred, I was directed by the Post Commander to prefer charges against the sentinel who allowed the prisoner to make good his escape, and I desire to say I am in no way prejudiced against the prisoner before the court, as I hardly have known him heretofore.

Q by prisoner: In framing the charges in this case did you not examine the witnesses?
A. I did not.
Q by prisoner: Of your own knowledge do you know anything material about the case or have you formed any opinion?
A. I know nothing at all, material, of the case and have not formed an opinion

1

2nd Day

9 O'clock A.M.   Fort Sill, I.T. July 10, 1873

The court met pursuant to the adjournment. Present all members of the Judge Advocate. In consequence of the presence of officers being required at the pay table to attend to the payment of the troops, the court adjourned until 9 O'clock A.M. on the 11th.

3rd Day

9 O'clock A.M.   Fort Sill, I.T. July 11, 1873

Present all the members except Capt. C. (?) F. Robe, 25th Infantry, the cause of whose absence in unknown. The Judge Advocate was also present. The Judge Advocate stated that he could not proceed with the case before the Court until the return of witnesses who are absent in the field, and requested the court to adjourn until 10 O'clock A.M. tomorrow to give him an opportunity to prepare another case. Therefore the court adjourned until 10 O'clock A.M. on the 12th instead

4th Day

10:30 O'clock A.M.   Fort Sill, July 25, 1873 (?)

The court met pursuant to adjournment. Present all the members and the Judge Advocate. The court then proceeded with the trial of Private Alfred Pride, Company B. 10th Cavalry, whose case was postponed on the 11th to await the return from the field of witnesses. The prisoner, Private Alfred Pride Co. B. 10th Cavalry was then brought before the Court. The Judge Advocate stated to the court that the prosecution rested its case on the evidence heretofore recorded.

Corporal Thomas Dilwood Co. B 10th Cavalry, a witness for the defence being duly sworn, deposes and says:

Q by prisoner: What is your name, rank, Co. and regiment?

A: Thomas Dilwood, Corporal Co. B 10th Cavalry

Q: Do you know me, and if so my name, rank, company and regiment?

A. Yes, Alfred Pride, Private Co. B 10th Cavalry

Q: Do you remember anything about a prisoner escaping from me at Ft. Gibson, and if so about when was it?

A. I don't remember exactly when, but it was in March 1873, one evening a prisoner got away from you.

Q. What was the prisoner's name who escaped?

A. His name was Davis of I Company 10th Cavalry.

Q: Where was the prisoner when he escaped from me?

A: I was not there when he escaped, the next morning I picked up his shackles in Captain Lawson's yard.

Q: Were the shackles broken or cut?

A. No

Q: How do you suppose he got them off?

A. He must have slipped them off.

Q: Do you suppose from this fact that they were too large for him?

A. Yes, they must have been too large.

Q. Were you Corporal of the Guard at that time?

A. Yes, the next day after the prisoner escaped.

3

Q. What instructions were given to the sentinels over prisoners?
A. The instructions turned over to me were that sentinels were to walk a beat ten paces from the prisoners, keep the prisoners at work and keep a cartridge in their belts.

Cross-examined
Q by Court: Are you positive the shackles you found were the shackles left by the prisoner?
A. No sir

Re-examined
Q by Prisoner: How far was the wood pile in Captain Lawson's yard from the gate where the prisoner is reported to have escaped through?
A. I can't say. I want not well enough acquainted with the place to tell.

The prisoner had no further testimony to offer and no statement to make. The court was then cleared and closed, and after mature deliberation upon the evidence adduced, find the prisoner Private Alfred Pride, Company B 10th Cavalry as follows;

Of the specification   "Not Guilty"
Of the charge   "Not Guilty"

And the court does therefore acquit him   ?, Captain   11th Infantry President

Head Quarters, Department of Texas   San Antonio, Texas   5 August 1873
In the case of Private Alfred Pride, Company B, 10th Cavalry, the record failing to set forth that the court and judge advocate were sworn, the proceedings are disapproved.

The reviewing authority concurring in the findings of the court, no further proceedings in this matter will be taken against the prisoner. Orders have already been issued for his release from confinement.
C.C. Augur (?)
Brigadier General ? Commanding

Court Martial of Sergeant Alfred Pride   Fort Robinson, Nebraska   October 17, 1890
Statement in case of Sergeant Alfred Pride, Troop K, 9th Regiment of U.S. Cavalry
Date of Present Enlistment: March 19, 1888
Date of former enlistments: 2nd enlistment: 11th of Feb 1873; 3rd enlistment: 11 Feb 1878; 4th
*   enlistment: March 10th 1883; 5th enlistment: March 19, 1888*
Character Given on Former Discharges: 4th enlistment Good, 2nd enlistment, Good (?), honest,
industrious, trusting soldier, 4th enlistment "Good"
Character at date: Good – is slow – does not comprehend readily
Date and Place of confinement for the offence covered by accompanying charges: Fort Robinson, Neb.
October 2, 1890
? Parker, Captain 9th Cavalry, Commanding Troop "K"

4

(Exhibit 2)

Transcript of Alfred Pride's Second Court Martial

Convened on October 17, 1890

Q. What instructions were given to the sentinels over prisoners?
A. The instructions turned over to me were that sentinels were to walk a beat ten paces from the prisoners, keep the prisoners at work and keep a cartridge in their belts.

Cross-examined
Q by Court: Are you positive the shackles you found were the shackles left by the prisoner?
A. No sir

Re-examined
Q by Prisoner: How far was the wood pile in Captain Lawson's yard from the gate where the prisoner is reported to have escaped through?
A. I can't say. I want not well enough acquainted with the place to tell.

The prisoner had no further testimony to offer and no statement to make. The court was then cleared and closed, and after mature deliberation upon the evidence adduced, find the prisoner Private Alfred Pride, Company B 10th Cavalry as follows;

Of the specification   "Not Guilty"
Of the charge   "Not Guilty"

And the court does therefore acquit him   ?, Captain   11th Infantry President

Head Quarters, Department of Texas   San Antonio, Texas   5 August 1873
In the case of Private Alfred Pride, Company B, 10th Cavalry, the record failing to set forth that the court and judge advocate were sworn, the proceedings are disapproved.

The reviewing authority concurring in the findings of the court, no further proceedings in this matter will be taken against the prisoner. Orders have already been issued for his release from confinement.
C.C. Augur (?)
Brigadier General ? Commanding

Court Martial of Sergeant Alfred Pride   Fort Robinson, Nebraska   October 17, 1890
Statement in case of Sergeant Alfred Pride, Troop K, 9th Regiment of U.S. Cavalry
Date of Present Enlistment: March 19, 1888
Date of former enlistments: 2nd enlistment: 11th of Feb 1873; 3rd enlistment: 11 Feb 1878; 4th
*   enlistment: March 10th 1883; 5th enlistment: March 19, 1888*
Character Given on Former Discharges: 4th enlistment Good, 2nd enlistment, Good (?), honest,
industrious, trusting soldier, 4th enlistment "Good"
Character at date: Good – is slow – does not comprehend readily
Date and Place of confinement for the offence covered by accompanying charges: Fort Robinson, Neb.
October 2, 1890
? Parker, Captain 9th Cavalry, Commanding Troop "K"

4

Fort Robinson, Neb. October 17, 1890

The Court met pursuant to the foregoing order at 10:30 O'clock A.M.

Present: Captain William S. Worth, 8th Infantry; Captain Clarence M. Bailey, 8th Infantry; Captain Charles Parker, 9th Cavalry; Captain Augustus W. Corliss, 8th Infantry; Captain George W. Adair, Ass't Surgeon, USA; Captain Clarence A. Stedman, 9th Cavalry; 1st Lieut. John J. Haden, 8th Infantry; 2nd Lieut. Alexander R. Piper, 8th Infantry; 1st Lieut. Edgar Hubert, 8th Infantry, Judge Advocate

Absent: Major Edgar R. Kellogg, 8th Infantry; Captain Martin B. Hughes, 9th Cavalry; 2nd Lieut. George W. Ruthers, 8th Infantry; 2nd Lieut. Colville M. Pettit, 8th Infantry; 2nd Lieut. Frank Owen, 8th Infantry.

Lieut. Pettit was absent on detached service. All the other absent officers have left this post under proper orders since this court was appointed.

The court then proceeded to the trial of Sergeant Alfred Pride, Troop K, 9 Cavalry who was brought before the court and, having heard the order convening it read, asked permission to introduce Captain F. B. Taylor, 9 Cavalry, as his counsel; the court assenting, the council took his seat.

The accused was then asked if he objected to being tried by any member present -- ....?.... – to which he replied in the negative. The accused pleaded "Not Guilty" to the specification and to the charge.

Private Albert Fowler, Co. C (?), 8th Infantry, a witness for the prosecution, was then duly sworn and testified as follows;

Questions by Judge Advocate:

Q. State your name and rank

A. Albert Fowler, Private, Co. C, 8th Infantry

Q. Do you know the accused?

A: I don't know his name, I know him by sight. I have seen him but once.

Q. When was that?

A: On guard a couple of weeks ago.

Q. Were you a prisoner in the guardhouse at that time?

A: Yes sir.

Q: Tell how it happened.

A: I was room orderly from the time I was arrested and I went into the next building to sweep out the rooms by order of the sergeant of the guard, and there was no one around and I went through the window.

Q. Who was the sergeant of the guard that gave you orders to go there?

A: That man yonder (pointing to the accused).

Q. Did he go with you or send any sentinel with you?

A: No sir. He came into the room a few minutes after he sent me there and asked me if I did any other work besides that – did I go out with the other prisoners. I told him I did not. He said it was all right.

Q. What did he do then?

A: He went away then.

Q. Where was all this?

A. At this post.

5

Q. Do you know upon what charges you were in the guardhouse at that time?
A: Yes sir, desertion

Cross Examination
Questions by accused:
Q: When were you first confined for desertion?
A: In September, the 14th or 15th I believe. About two weeks before I escaped.
Q. Who put you on duty as room orderly at the guardhouse?
A: The Sergeant of the Guard, I believe it was Gillise (?)
Q. What was your purpose in leaving the guardhouse that morning?
A: My purpose was to go.
Q: Are you aware that your running away from the guard that morning laid you liable to a second charge of desertion?
A: No sir
Q by Court: What time of day was it that you escaped?
A: In the morning about 7:30 or 8 o'clock.
Q by Court: Was there any confusion going on in the garrison about the time of your escape?
A: Yes sir, the troops were getting ready to go down town.
Q by Court: What is the building used for that you were cleaning up?
A: It is used for the guard and prisoners.
Q by Court: Did you escape from the guard room or the prison room?
A: From the guard room.

The testimony of the witness was then read to him and pronounced correct. Corporal John Thomas, Troop F, 9th Cavalry, a witness for the prosecution, was then duly sworn and testified as follows:

Questions by Judge Advocate
Q. State your name and rank
A: John Thomas, Corporal, Troop F, 9th Cavalry
Q. Do you know the accused?
A: I know him if I see him, but I don't know his name.
Q. Were you on guard with him the day that Fowler escaped from the guard house?
A: Yes sir
Q: Did you have any encounters about Fowler?
A: Yes sir
Q: What was it?
A: I asked Sergeant Pride where Fowler was. He said he was out there to the house where he said he was at. I came back and told him that the prisoner wasn't there. He said he was because he had left him about two minutes before.
Q. Where was the prisoner, Sergeant Pride, when this conversation took place?
A: He was in the rear – in the privy.

The accused declined to cross-examine this witness. The testimony of the witness was then read to him and pronounced correct. First Lieutenant E. Hubert, 8th Infantry, a witness for the prosecution, was then duly sworn and testified as follows:

6

Questions by Judge Advocate

Q: Were you on guard with Sergeant Pride on October 2, 1890?

A: I was.

Q: Were you relieved from guard before your tour was completed?

A: I was relieved at reveille on October 2 at 6 o'clock – by the officer of the day in order to attend the meeting of the Grand Army at Crawford. When I left I told Sergeant Pride to take charge of the guard, that I would not be back any more.

The Judge Advocate announced that the prosecution had rested. The accused declined to cross-examine the last witness.

Private Thomas Loper (?), Troop F, 9th Cavalry, a witness for the defense, was then duly sworn and testified as follows:

Q: Were you on guard with Sergeant Pride when Fowler ran away?

A: Yes sir

Q. What number was your fort?

A: Number 7 of the 20 Relief (?)

Q: When were you on post that morning?

A: From 5 until 7 o'clock.

Q: Did you see Sergeant Pride leave the guard house to go to breakfast?

A: Yes sir

Q: Where was Fowler when the Sergeant left?

A: In the main guard room where the guard stays.

Q: Did you see Fowler go to work at – work cleaning up the guard house?

A: Yes sir

Q. Was this before Sergeant Pride returned from breakfast?

A: Yes sir

Q: Were you warned by any one of the character of Fowler, that he was a prisoner liable to escape if possible?

A: No sir

Q: Was Fowler in ___?

A: No sir

Q. Who relieved you off of post?

A: Corporal Whaley, Co. C, 8th Infantry

Cross-Examination

Questions by Judge Advocate

Q: Which guardhouse did you see him go to work in before Sergeant Pride returned from breakfast?

A: In the old adjutant's office

Q: Who took him there?

A: No one.

Q by court: What are the orders for No. 1 in regard to prisoners leaving the guardhouse? Is not No. 1 required to see that they are accompanied by a sentinel?

A. I had no orders to stop him from leaving the guardhouse. Yes to the first part of the question.

Q by court: Did you have any orders to the contrary in this case?

7

A: No sir

The testimony of the witness was then read to him and pronounced correct. Private Benjamin Davis, Troop I (?), 9th Cavalry, a witness for the defense, was then duly sworn and testified as follows:
Questions by accused:
Q. When you were on guard the morning Fowler escaped, did you notice Sergeant Pride going to breakfast?
A: Yes sir
Q. Did you see Fowler working about the guardhouse that morning?
A: Yes sir
Q: Where was Sergeant Pride when Fowler commenced to work?
A: He was to breakfast
Q: Did you know anything about the character of Prisoner Fowler, whether or not he was liable to escape?
A. No sir

The testimony of the witness was then read to him and pronounced correct. The accused was then, at his own request, duly sworn and testified in his own defense as follows:

Questions by Accused:
Q. Have you been doing post guard duty regularly on this post?
A: No sir, I haven't done any since Feb '88.
Q: Was Prisoner Fowler turned over to you as a prisoner specifically to be watched and guarded – that he was likely to escape?
A: No sir
Q: Did you not see from the guard book when you made out the report that he was charged with desertion?
A: No sir. I didn't notice the guard report because Corporal Whaley is a better scribe than I am and I got him to make it out.
Q: Did you sit (?) Fowler to work cleaning out the guardhouse?
A: No sir. When I came back from breakfast, he was in the old office of the guard room sweeping. I asked him what he was doing there and he said he was room orderly and I went to the rear. While I was in the rear Corporal Thomas came in and asked me where was the prisoner. I told him he was in the room sweeping out, that I hadn't left him more than about two minutes and a half before. He told me he was gone. I went and reported the case to the officer of the guard and he directed me to report to the officer of the day. Then I went back to the guardhouse and taken a horse of my troop to hunt for him. I rode up and down White River one each side in the bushes. I came back and went towards town. I met Private Boone and he told me he met a man crossing a bridge going towards town. He had on a canvas coat and red necktie and gray hat and a pair of barrack shoes and a pair of blue trousers. This ___? the description of Fowler and I went on and met two citizens in the road who told me they arrested him and taken him to camp.
Q: Why did you leave Fowler alone in the room when you went to the rear?
A: He was room orderly and I didn't know at that time he was a general prisoner.
Q. How long have you been in the service? State your service as a soldier?
A: I have been in the service twenty-two and a half years. This is my fifth enlistment

8

Q by court: When you went to breakfast did you turn the guard over to the next non-commissioned officer of the guard?
A: Yes sir

The testimony of the witness was then read to him and pronounced correct. Captain Charles Parker, 9th Cavalry, a witness for the defense, was then duly sworn and testified as follows:

Q by Accused: Please tell to the court what is my character as a soldier, and how long I have been in the service, if you know?
A: The first that I knew of him was at Fort Supply in F Company, 24th Infantry, about two years ago. Then he re-enlisted in K Troop, 9th Cavalry, my troop. He served in to about five years and one morning he came to me and said he wanted to be a non-commissioned officer. It rather amused me and I told him I would try him as a corporal. He has served as a non-commissioned officer since. He has been jumped over one or two times as a non-commissioned officer, but I have never found anything so serious as to prevent his being a sergeant. He is honest and faithful as far as he knows. The chief point I have found about his is that he is rather slow to comprehend. I believe he tries to do the best he can.
Q by Accused: What character was given him on his discharges?
A: All good

The testimony of the witness was then read to him and pronounced correct. The court then at 3 o'clock adjourned to meet at 10:30 o'clock A.M. on October 20, 1890.

Fort Robinson, Nebraska October 21, 1890
Captain Charles Parker, 9th Cavalry, has left this post under proper orders since the last meeting of the Court in this case. The accused and his counsel were also present.

The accused then submitted his final defense which was read to the Court by his counsel and is hereto appended and marked "A". The Judge Advocate submitted the case without remark. The court was then cleared and closed for deliberation and having maturely considered the evidence adduced finds the accused Sergeant Alfred Pride, Troop K, 9 Cav.
Of Specification   Guilty
Of Charge   Guilty

And the court does therefore sentence Sergeant Alfred Pride, Troop K, 9 Cav. to be reduced to the rank of private soldier and to forfeit ten ($10) dollars per month of his pay for two (2) months. The court is thus lenient on account of his long service and good character as shown in evidence.

The court then at 11:15 o'clock A.M. proceeded to other business.

"A" (Written statement from Sgt. Pride)
May it please the Court, I will detain you but a brief statement. I have shown that I was ignorant of the character of the prisoner Fowler, of what he was confined for, or that he was likely to try to escape from the guard. On the contrary, finding him acting as room orderly naturally lead me to suppose him to be a garrison prisoner. For it has been my experience that only such prisoners are

9

even selected for that duty. And the corporal made out the guard report that day kept me from learning differently. Besides I had done no post guard duty for eight months and I had no opportunity to learn anything about the prisoners in the guard house.

The statement of the prisoner that it was I who set him at work that morning without a guard is disproved by witnesses Loffer (?) and Davis, as well be seen by reference to their testimony. I only .....
{record ended here}

HEADQUARTERS DEPARTMENT OF THE PLATTE   Omaha, Nebraska, October 25, 1890
Sergeant Alfred Pride, Troop K, 9th Cavalry
Charge: "Neglect of duty, in violation of the 62d Article of War".
Specification: "That he, Sergeant Alfred Pride, Troop K, 9th Cavalry, being duly detailed as sergeant of the post guard, did, while in charge of said guard, permit Private Alfred Fowler, Company C, 8th Infantry, a prisoner, to escape. This at Fort Robinson, Neb., and on or about the 2d of October, 1890.
Pleas: "Not Guilty"
Findings: "Guilty"
Sentence: "*To be reduced to the rank of private soldier, and to forfeit ten ($10.00) per month of his pay for two months. The court is thus lenient on account of his long service and good character as shown in evidence*".

The proceedings, findings and sentence in the case of Sergeant Alfred Pride, Troop K, 9th Cavalry, are approved, and the sentence will be duly executed. Private Pride will be released from arrest and returned to duty.

By Command of Brigadier General Brooke:
M.V. Sheridan, Ass't Adjutant General

10

(Exhibit 3)

Dr. Taylor Meets Troopers Crawford and Hillat

Dr. Alfred O. Taylor, Jr., Great Grandson of Trooper Alfred Pride with Troopers Crawford
and Hillat Drew Model Elementary School Presentation April 12, 2012

(Exhibit 4)

Alfred Pride's Service Records

Enlisted 10 February 1868 in Boston at age 22
- Servant
- 10th Cavalry B
- Expiration of Service at Ft. Gibson, Indian Territory
- Black, Black, Black 5'6"

Arrival at Post: 13 January 1869. Fort Lyons
- Remarks: Sick
- 10th Cavalry K

Date of Arrival at Post: 14 June 1869
- 10th Cavalry B
- On extra duty when his company marched to Medicine Bluff Creek (?) from Ft. Dodge

Troops Leaving Fort Duncan, Texas 11 February 1878
- Left at this fort with discharge for signature of commanding office and final statements completed and signed
- 10th Cavalry B
- Company B 10th Cavalry left Fort February ? 1878 and ordered to take station at Fort Stockton; Headquarters of Texas, January 26, 1878
- Relieved of duty at this Fort ... Fort Duncan (?), Texas Feburary 4/11, 1878

Enlisted 11 February 1878 at Ft. Duncan at age 32
- 24th Infantry Company F
- Number of enlistments: 3
- Discharged 10 February 1883
- Expiration of Service at Ft. Elliott, Texas
- Character: Good
- Black, Black, Brown

Enlisted 11 July 1878 at Ft. Robinson at age 32
- 10th Cavalry B
- Discharge 10 July 1883
- Expiration of service Fort Elliott, Texas
- Black, Black, Brown 5'8"

Enlisted 10 March 1883 in St. Louis at the age 37
- 9th Cavalry Troop K
- Discharged 9 March 1888 at Ft. Robinson
- Character Good

Enlisted 10 March 1888 at Fort Robinson at age 42
- 9th Cavalry K
- Five enlistments
- Discharged 9 March 1893
- Expiration of Service at Fort Myer

(Exhibit 5)

Register of Enlistments

313

REGISTER OF ENLISTMENTS,

NO.	NAMES.		1888 ENLISTED.				WHERE BORN.		AGE.	OCCUPATION.	DESCRIPTION.			
			WHEN.	WHERE.	BY WHOM.	PERIOD.	TOWN OR COUNTY.	STATE.			EYES.	HAIR.	COMPLEXION.	
42	Perry	George	February 11	St Louis Mo	Capt Morgan	5 Yrs	Dubois Co	Ind	21	Cook	Bro	Bro	Dark	5
3	Proctor	Thomas	" 13	Ft Lewis W.T.	Lieut McWeeks	"	Montgomery Co	Ill	27	Soldier	Black	Black	Dark	5
4	Pladal	Charles	" 7	Albany N.Y.	Capt Rodman	"	Albany	N.Y.	24	Waiter	Hazel	Bro	Dark	5
5	Phillips	John	" 25	New York City	Role	"	Frankfort	Germany	25	Fireman	Bro	Dk Bro	"	5
6	Parker	John S	" 11	Annapolis Md	Smith	"	Annapolis	Md	33	Laborer	Black	Black	Black	5
7	Peterson	George	" 21	Quincy Ills	Thibat	"	Baden	Germany	21	Tailor	Hazel	"	Dark	5
8	Pritchard	Appleton	" 10	Mt Vernon Bks	Lieut Thompson	"	Fredericksburg	Va	37	Soldier	Bro	Light	Fair	5
9	Petrie	Samuel	March 1	Memphis Tenn	Borden	"	Madison Co	Ala	21	Laborer	Black	Black	Dark	5
50	Powell	Robert	" 23			"	Memphis	Tenn	24				Black	5
1	Pearsall	Willis	" 19	Ft Sill I.T.	Brereton	"	Carter Co	Ky	22	Soldier			Yellow	5
2	Pierce	Wellington	" 30	Newark N.J.	Carter	"	Hunterstown	Penna	21	Baker	Grey	Light	Ruddy	5
3	Prince	Frank D	" 24	Presidio St Cal	Cotton	"	Clarence	N.Y.	35	Soldier	"	Dk Bro	Fair	5
4	Pickard	John A	" 12	Ft Bayard N.M.	Craig	"	Elberfield	Prussia	26		Bro	Light		5
5	Peckham	George	" 9	Buffalo N.Y.	Capt Crindell	"	Oneida	N.Y.	21	Laborer	"	Black	Dark	5
6	Polka	Henry	" 26			"	Napoleon	O	23		Grey	Bro	Fair	5
7	Pietsch	Charles	" 26	Chicago Ills	Godwin	"	Mecklenburg	Germany	21		Hazel	"	Ruddy	5
8	Peterson	John	" 1			"	Nora	Sweden	31		Blue	Light	Fair	5
9	Porter	Rufus R	" 8	Ft Caswell Minn	Garrelly	"	Calais	Me	21		"	Dark	Dark	5
60	Pederson	Martin	" 20			"	Hammer	Norway	23		"	Light	Fair	5
1	Pride	Alfred	" 10	Ft Watson Nebr	Lieut Guilfoyle	"	Richmond	Va	42	Soldier	Black	Black	Black	5
2	Potter	George E	" 23	Camden N.J.	Kaye	"	Cleveland	O	20	Laborer	Blue	Bro	Fair	5
3	Plass	Alexander H	" 13	Charleston S.C.	Hutton	"	Gestemunde	Germany	21	Clerk	Grey	Lt Bro	Light	5
4	Pederson	Christian	" 21	Walkerman St	Anstriel	"		Denmark	25	Soldier	Blue	Light	Fair	5
5	Ponder	John	" 10	St Augustine	Hoyle	"	Jackson	Ga	27	Laborer	Bro	Bro	"	5
6	Pheasant	Samuel J	" 8	Baltimore Md	Capt Auguin	"	Caseville	Pa	27	Fireman	Hazel	"	"	5
7	Pritchard	Frank	" 13	Ft Omaha Neb	Lieut Kingie	"	St Marys	O	35	Druggist	Bro	Black	"	5
8	Petti	Charles G	" 23	New York N.Y.	Lewis	"	Philadelphia	Pa	24	Soldier	Hazel	Bro	"	5
9	Phillips	William	" 14	Baltimore Md	Mumford	"	Essex Co	Va	23	Laborer	Bro	Black	Bro	5
70	Porter	Abraham	" 5			"	Baltimore	Md	23				Mulatto	5
1	Palmer	Will A	" 6	Ft Keio I.T.	Mickler	"	Berks Co	Pa	41	Soldier	Grey	"	Light	5
2	Platner	George	" 16	St Louis Mo	Capt Morgan	"	Bohemia	Austria	27	Clerk	Blue	"	Fair	5
3	Poggstert	Edward	" 26			"	St Louis	Mo	24					5
4	Payne	John E	" 17	Fort Riley Kas	Lieut McComb	"	Crawford Co	Ills	22	Laborer	Gray	"	"	5
5	Powers	William	" 5	San Francisco Cal	Rice	"	Baltimore	Md	37	Soldier	Blue	"	Ruddy	5
6	Pinder	William J	" 19	Albany N.Y.	Capt Rodman	"	Cohoes	N.Y.	27		"	Black	"	5
7	Parle	John	" 1	San Antonio Tex	Richards	"	Newford	Ireland	49		Grey	Grey	Dark	5
8	Pink	Robert J	" 3	Philadelphia Pa	Lieut Scott	"	Cleveland	O	23	Organ Tuner	"	Light	Fair	5
9	Parker	George	" 31			"	Germantown	Pa	22	Carpenter	"	Bro	Sallow	5
80	Pickens	Edward	" 12	Ft Verde A.T.	Smith	"	Tuscaloosa	Ala	26	Soldier	Black	Black	Black	5
1	Plankham	William W	" 16	Quincy Ills	Thibat	"	Columbus	O	31	Farmer	Bro	Dk Bro	Fair	5
2	Penwell	George B	" 28	Philadelphia Pa	Vernon	"	Philadelphia	Pa	39	Soldier	Grey	Bro	"	5

REGIMENT.	CO.	No. of Enlistment.				REMARKS.				

	K		Des May 4.88							
	G	Enl.	Disch'd Feb. 12/93, Expr. of Ser., Ft. Missoula, Mont. Prt. None.							
	C		Disch'd May 2/91, S.O. 15, Dept. Dak. 91, Ft. Randall, S.D., a Prt. Char. Exclt.							
Eng.	B		Des June 15.88							
	K		Disch'd Feb. 10/93, Expr. of Ser., Ft. Custer Mont. Prt. Good							
	K.F.		Disch'd Feb. 20/93, Expr. of Ser., Ft. Sam Houston, Texas, Prt. Very good							
Fo.	4		Disch'd Sept. 26/91, S.O. 213, A.G.O. 91, Ft. Brown, Texas, a Sergt. Char. Exclt.							
	M.B.		Disch'd Feb. 25/93, Expr. of Ser., Ft. DuChesne, U.T., Corpl. Exclt.							
y	G		Disch'd Mch. 22/93, Expr. of Ser., Ft. Missoula, Mont. Prt. Good							
y	C	3	Disch'd Mch. 18/93, Expr. of Ser., Ft. Bayard, N.M., Artificer Good							
	A		Des. Disch'gd Mch. 21. 89 for Glo.M.O. 23 Dept. of Dak. 89 at Ft. Meade Dak. a Prt.							
	N.	3	Disch'd Apr. 12/93, Expr. of Ser., Ft. Leavenworth, Kan., Art. Good.-					Ret'd in Ser.	
	M	2	Des Feby 17/90							
	G		Disch'd Mch. 8/93, Expr. of Ser., Angel Isld, Cal., Prt. Good							
2 Inf.	C.A.		Disch'd Mch. 25/93, Expr. of Ser., Ft. Omaha, Neb., Prt. Very good							
			Des July 17.88 at Jeff Bks Mo							
y	D.		Des Disch'gd Aug. 20 89 for Glo.M.O. 8 Dept. of Col. 89 at Vanc. Bks. W.T. a Prt. N. Char							
y	L&C		Disch'd June 1/91, S.O. 37, Dept. Dak. 91, Camp on Nez Perces Creek, Wyo., a Sergt Char. Exclt.							
y	C.		Disch'd June 14/91, G.O. 80, A.G.O. 90, Ft. Leavenworth, Kan., a Corpl. Char. Exclt.							
y	K.	5	Disch'd Mch. 9/93, Expr. of Ser., Ft. Myer, Va., Prt. Good							
	G		Des Nov 11.88							
	N		Disch'gd July 13 88 for Disability at Ft. Walla Walla W.T. a Prt. Char Fair							50 real
	C.	2	Disch'd Dec. 17/92, Disability, Ft. Spokane, Wash., Prt. Char. Very good							D.C.
4 Arty	D.C		Disch'd Mch. 9/93, Expr. of Ser., Ft. McPherson, Ga., Prt. Exclt.							
	F.		Des Aug 10. 88							
	J.		Des Apl 25.88 Surd Jany 5. 89 Disch'gd June 5 89, to date Apl 25.88 at Newport Bks My for Ft Ins from R.E.O 59 vds 4 No 4 C.B. 89 a Prt							Char Mony
	B.		Disch'gd Nov 3 89 for Disability at Ft Wood N.Y. a Prt. Char Fair							50 real
	C.		Disch'd June 13/91, G.O. 80, A.G.O. 90, Ft. Shaw, Mont., a Prt. Char. Good.							
y	C.		Disch'd May 28/92, Disability, Ft. Buford, N.D., a Corpl. Char., Exclt.							D.C. recd.
	O.	5	Disch'd Mch. 5/93, Expr. of Ser., Ft. Reno, O.T., Sergt. Exclt.							
	L		Disch'd June 16/91, G.O. 80, A.G.O. 90, Ft. Walla Walla, Wash., a Prt. Char. Good							
	B.		Disch'd Mch. 25/93, Ft. Meade, S.D. Farrier, Exclt.							
	G.		Disch'd June 16/91, G.O. 80, A.G.O. 90, Ft. Clark, Texas, a Prt. Char. Exclt.							
✓	M.	2	Des Mch 11 89							
	K	2	Disch'd Mch. 18/93, Expr. of Ser., Ft. Leavenworth Kan., Prt. Very good							
y	G.	6	Disch'd Feb. 28/93, Expr. of Ser., Ft. Douglas, Utah, Prt. Very good							
			Des. Apl. 6.88 at Jeff Bks Mo							
	L.		Des Apl 17/90							
y	J.	6.	Disch'd June 11/91, S.O. 80, A.G.O. 90, Ft. Apache, A.T., Sergt. Char. Exclt.							
			Disch'gd May 2.88 at Col Bks. O for S.O. 98 A.G.O. 88 a Rect. Char. Fair							
	D.	4.	Disch'd Oct. 17/90, S.O. 232, A.G.O. 90, Jackson Bks, La., a Mus'n. Char. Exclt.							

(Exhibit 6)

Alfred Pride's Service Record

Pride Service Records

Enlisted 10 February 1868 in Boston at age 22
- Servant
- 10th Cavalry B
- Expiration of Service at Ft. Gibson, Indian Territory
- Black, Black, Black 5'6"

Arrival at Post: 13 January 1869. Fort Lyons
- Remarks: Sick
- 10th Cavalry K

Date of Arrival at Post: 14 June 1869
- 10th Cavalry B
- On extra duty when his company marched to Medicine Bluff Creek (?) from Ft. Dodge

Troops Leaving Fort Duncan, Texas 11 February 1878
- Left at this fort with discharge for signature of commanding office and final statements completed and signed
- 10th Cavalry B
- Company B 10th Cavalry left Fort February ? 1878 and ordered to take station at Fort Stockton; Headquarters of Texas, January 26, 1878
- Relieved of duty at this Fort ... Fort Duncan (?), Texas Feburary 4/11, 1878

Enlisted 11 February 1878 at Ft. Duncan at age 32
- 24th Infantry Company F
- Number of enlistments: 3
- Discharged 10 February 1883
- Expiration of Service at Ft. Elliott, Texas
- Character: Good
- Black, Black, Brown

Enlisted 11 July 1878 at Ft. Robinson at age 32
- 10th Cavalry B
- Discharge 10 July 1883
- Expiration of service Fort Elliott, Texas
- Black, Black, Brown 5'8"

Enlisted 10 March 1883 in St. Louis at the age 37
- 9th Cavalry Troop K
- Discharged 9 March 1888 at Ft. Robinson
- Character Good

Enlisted 10 March 1888 at Fort Robinson at age 42
- 9th Cavalry K
- Five enlistments
- Discharged 9 March 1893
- Expiration of Service at Fort Myer

- Black, Black, Black 5'8"

<u>Enlisted March 10, 1893 at Fort Meyer at 47</u>
- 9th Cavalry K
- Six enlistments
- Last Service: K9 9 March 1893
- Prob: Very Good

(Exhibit 7)

Alfred Pride's Service Record

U.S., Buffalo Soldiers, Returns From Regular Army Cavalry Regiments, 1866-1916 - Ancestry.com

Alford Pride
in the U.S., Buffalo Soldiers, Returns From Regular Army Cavalry Regiments, 1866-1916

Name:	Alford Pride
Regiment:	United States Tenth Cavalry
Regiment Return Date:	Feb 1873
Regiment Commanding Officer:	B H Grierson
Officer or Enlisted:	Enlisted
Rank:	Private
Company Letter:	B
Number:	10
Action Date:	10 Feb 1873
Action Place:	Indian Territory
Roll Number:	96
Archive Publication Number:	M744
Archive Publication Title:	Returns From Regular Army Cavalry Regiments 1866-1916

Source Citation
Washington, D.C.; *National Archives and Records Administration (NARA)*

(Exhibit 8)

Alfred Pride's Service Record

U.S., Buffalo Soldiers, Returns From Regular Army Cavalry Regiments, 1866-1916 - Ancestry.com

A Pride
in the U.S., Buffalo Soldiers, Returns From Regular Army Cavalry Regiments, 1866-1916

Name:	A Pride
Regiment:	United States Tenth Cavalry
Regiment Return Date:	Mar 1869
Regiment Commanding Officer:	Colonel B H Grierson
Officer or Enlisted:	Enlisted
Rank:	Private
Company Letter:	B
Action Place:	Fort Lyon, Colorado Territory
Roll Number:	95
Archive Publication Number:	M744
Archive Publication Title:	Returns From Regular Army Cavalry Regiments 1866-1916

Source Citation
Washington, D.C.; *National Archives and Records Administration (NARA)*

(Exhibit 9)

Alfred Pride's Service Record

U.S., Buffalo Soldiers, Returns From Regular Army Cavalry Regiments, 1866-1916 - Ancestry.com

ancestry

Alfred Pride
in the U.S., Buffalo Soldiers, Returns From Regular Army Cavalry Regiments, 1866-1916

Name:	Alfred Pride
Regiment:	United States Tenth Cavalry
Regiment Return Date:	Apr 1868
Regiment Commanding Officer:	Colonel And Brevet Major General B H Grierson
Officer or Enlisted:	Enlisted
Rank:	Private
Company Letter:	B
Number:	1
Action Date:	1 Apr 1868
Action Place:	Fort Riley, Kansas
Roll Number:	95
Archive Publication Number:	M744
Archive Publication Title:	Returns From Regular Army Cavalry Regiments 1866-1916

Source Citation
Washington, D.C.; *National Archives and Records Administration (NARA)*

(Exhibit 10)

Alfred Pride's Service Record

U.S., Buffalo Soldiers, Returns From Regular Army Cavalry Regiments, 1866-1916 - Ancestry.com

ncestry

Alfred Pride
in the U.S., Buffalo Soldiers, Returns From Regular Army Cavalry Regiments, 1866-1916

Name:	Alfred Pride
Regiment:	United States Tenth Cavalry
Regiment Return Date:	Mar 1873
Regiment Commanding Officer:	B H Grierson
Officer or Enlisted:	Enlisted
Rank:	Private
Company Letter:	B
Number:	11
Action Date:	12 Mar 1873
Action Place:	Indian Territory
Roll Number:	96
Archive Publication Number:	M744
Archive Publication Title:	Returns From Regular Army Cavalry Regiments 1866-1916

Source Citation
Washington, D.C.; *National Archives and Records Administration (NARA)*

(Exhibit 11)

Alfred Pride's Service Record

U.S., Returns from Military Posts, 1806-1916 - Ancestry.com

Alfred Pride
in the U.S., Returns from Military Posts, 1806-1916

Name:	Alfred Pride
Post Name:	Supply, Fort
Post Location:	Oklahoma
Post Commander:	Nelson
Military Place:	Camp Supply, Indian Territory
Return Period:	Jul 1869

rds Administration (NARA); Washington, D.C.; *Returns from U.S. Military Posts, 1800-1916*; Microfilm Serial: *M617*; Microfilm Roll: *1243*

(Exhibit 12)

Battle of Rattlesnake Springs

Bruce J. Dinges General

RATTLESNAKE SPRINGS, BATTLE OF. On August 6, 1880, forty miles north of the site of present Van Horn, black soldiers of the Tenth United States Cavalry and a detachment of the Twenty-fourth United States Infantry fought Victorio in the climactic engagement of the Apache leader's incursion into West Texas. Since leaving the Mescalero Reservation near Fort Stanton, New Mexico, the previous August, the Apaches had raided back and forth across the international boundary, pillaging settlements in Chihuahua and New Mexico and causing alarm in the remote reaches of Texas. In late July 1880 Victorio and 125 to 150 of his followers crossed the Rio Grande, intending either to return to the vicinity of their former reservation or to find refuge in the rugged Guadalupe Mountains on the Texas-New Mexico border. Col. Benjamin H. Grierson, commanding the Tenth Cavalry and the District of the Pecos, decided not to pursue Victorio, but rather stationed troops at strategic waterholes and crossings, knowing that the Indians could not pass through the dry Trans-Pecos without water. On July 30 he repulsed the band at the battle of Tinaja de las Palmas, south of the site of present Sierra Blanca. Victorio withdrew into Mexico to regroup, but soon reappeared north of the river.

On August 3 Cpl. Asa Weaver of Company H, Tenth Cavalry, and a small detail of soldiers and scouts skirmished with the Indians near Alamo Springs between the Eagle and Van Horn mountains. That evening Grierson marched northeast from Eagle Springs to intercept the Apaches near Van Horn's Wells. Learning that Victorio had veered off to the northwest, at 3 A.M. on August 5 Grierson broke camp ten miles southeast of the wells and set out in pursuit with five companies of the Tenth Cavalry, numbering 170 officers and men. Capt. John C. Gilmore and twenty-five men of Company H, Twenty-fourth Infantry, remained behind to protect the supply train. Screened by mountains on the west, the cavalry paralleled the Indians' line of march, covering sixty-five miles in less than twenty-one hours. Around midnight the troopers arrived at Rattlesnake Springs, in the broad valley that separates the Sierra Diablo on the west and the Delaware and Apache mountains on the east. Remarkably, the cavalrymen had outmarched their fast-moving foe. Colonel Grierson, accompanied by his seventeen-year-old son, Robert, aide-de-camp Lt. William H. Beck, surgeon B. F. Kingsley, two ambulances, and a wagon, caught up with his command at 3:30 A.M. on August 6 and set up camp at the spring. Evidently Grierson took no direct part in the subsequent engagement.

The fight on August 6 unfolded haphazardly. While Capt. Nicholas Nolan's Company A scouted the passes through the mountains, Capt. Charles Viele positioned companies C and G in Rattlesnake Canyon guarding the approaches to the spring. At two o'clock in the afternoon, his men opened fire at a distance and halted the cautious advance of Victorio's warriors. The Indians reorganized and were working their way around the soldiers when Capt. Louis H. Carpenter appeared on the scene with companies H and B and drove them back into the hills and arroyos. About 4 P.M. Captain Gilmore and the supply train rounded a point of mountains to the southeast. A small party of Indians attacked the wagons, but quickly withdrew under fire from the infantry and cavalry escort. An attempt to scatter the soldiers' packmules near the springs likewise failed, and Victorio retreated into the mountains. Pvt. Wesley Hardy of Company H, Tenth Cavalry, was reported missing in the engagement, and some sources reported that possibly three other troops were killed. Reports on Indian losses varied from four killed to up to thirty casualties for the combined fight at Tinaja and Rattlesnake Springs.

Although scarcely more than a skirmish, the fight at Rattlesnake Springs was important in convincing Victorio to abandon the Trans-Pecos. On August 7 Capt. Thomas C. Lebo reported to Grierson that four days earlier his Company K had located and destroyed the Indians' supply camp in the Sierra Diablo. Twice defeated, hungry, and denied access to water holes, Victorio abandoned his effort to return to New Mexico and fled back across the Rio Grande. On October 15 Mexican forces killed him in the Tres Castillos Mountains. Victorio's death ended the Indian threat to West Texas.

(Exhibit 13)

Fort Myer, Virginia

Buffalo Soldiers at Fort Myer, Virginia

From 1891 to 1894, the Buffalo Soldiers of Troop (Company) K of the 9th Cavalry Regiment were stationed at Fort Myer. The pictured had no names of those featured.

Again, I can only wonder, if one of them is Alfred Pride.

(Exhibit 14)

Record of Troop B Skirmishes

April 10-29, 1876: Troops B, E, and F, bordering Coahiilla, Mexico, scouted unknown territory without guides. They describe the country as the roughest and most desolate land they had ever seen. It was without any value, in anyway.

August 12th: Troops B, E, and K, in the Santa Rosa Mountains of Mexico, destroyed an Indian village and its' supplies. Sixty horses were captured in the raid.

November-December 1876 Company at Ft. Clark, Texas: Colonel Grierson put Companies A, B, D, E, F, K, L on patrol in the Pecos River area and in the Guadalupe Mountains, scattering small bands of Indians.

January4, 1877: Troops B, D, and F struck the camp of Indian cattle thieves in the Santa Rosa Mountains, Mexico. The hostiles retreated, leaving a great amount of equipment, which was destroyed.

January 10th, 1877: Santa Rosa Mountains: Captain Keyes of the Tenth with Troops B and D and Lieutenant Bullis and his Seminole-Negro Indian Scouts, were on escort duty. After its completion, they marched from Fort Clark into Mexico in pursuit of the Lipan and Kickapoo Indians. They destroyed an abandoned Indian camp and returned to Fort Clark January, 23rd. February 2nd, the Company left Ft. Clark and arrived at Ft. Concho on February 11, 1877.

February-March, 1877, Santa Rosa Mountains: More incursions into these mountains results in destruction of more abandoned Indian camps by Troops B, D, and F of the Tenth. While on one of the expeditions, Sergeant Sandy Winchester of Troop F, was accidentally shot and killed.

(Exhibit 15)

Alfred Pride's Service Record

"On the Trail of the Buffalo Soldier II" by Irene Schubert, Frank N. Schubert, page 232

Pride, Alfred; Private; K/9th Calvary
Born and reared in Amelia Court House, VA, near Richmond; occupation laborer; ran away from home at age 16; enlisted Washington, DC 1865; appointed Sergeant, Fort Robinson, NE, K/9th Calvary, 1 July 1888; married Matilda Hawkins of Washington, age 32, in Washington 5 May 1898; first marriage for both; resided in Washington 30 years   Source: *VA File WC 10020, Alfred Pride*

Private, B/10th Calvary, transferred to Ft. Sill, IT *(Indian Country)*
Source: Special Order 57, HQ, DET 10 Calvary, Camp Supply   Indian Territory, 10 August 1869

At Ft. Duncan, TX 1877, with assistance of Lt. John Bigelow wrote letter of complaint to paymaster about not receiving pay for six months   Source: *Kinevan, Frontier Calvaryman, 60-61*

Sergeant, K/9th Calvary and sergeant of guard, Fort Robinson, when he allowed prisoner to escape and was reduced to private and fined $20: "But for his long service and good character the sentence would have been more severe."   Source: *ANJ 28 (18 November 1890): 120*

Widow Matilda Pride received $12 per month pension as of 4 March 1917; resided at 2600 I Street NW, Washington, when she died 20 March 1928 with a pension of $30 per month; last husband served in B/10th Calvary, F/24th Infantry, 1878-1883 and K/9th Calvary, 1883-98; he died of apoplexy in Washington, 2 August 1910; buried at Arlington Cemetery 5 August 1910 Source: *VA File WC 10020, Alfred Pride*

Survived by brother George Allen Pride, messenger, Department of Treasury, 1237 22nd Street NW, Washington; also brother John Henry Pride, blacksmith, Amelia Court House; brother Moses, laborer, 1411 Massachusetts Avenue NW, Washington; sister Mary Ann, wife of farmer Eugene Morton, Rumney, NH   Source: *VA File WC 10020, Alfred Pride*

(Exhibit 16)

Buffalo Soldiers at Fort Elliott

By Bill Kirchner, March 17, 2016

1. Buffalo Soldiers at Fort Elliott Marker

Inscription. Fort Elliott, established June 5, 1875 to help keep Native Americans on their Indian territory reservations, was partially garrisoned by African American soldiers called "Buffalo Soldiers" by Native Americans. Various companies of the 9th and 10th Cavalry and the 24th and 25th Infantry were stationed at Fort Elliott in its fifteen-year existence. Typical post duties included patrolling the boundary between Texas and Indian territory, keeping order among settlers, protecting mail coaches, and building roads and telegraph lines. Commanding officers of the troops were White, but the Black soldiers were included in every part of daily and social post life.

One Black officer stationed at Fort Elliott was Henry O. Flipper, commissioned as a second lieutenant in 1877. Born of slave parents in 1856, he was the first Black graduate of the United States Military Academy and the first

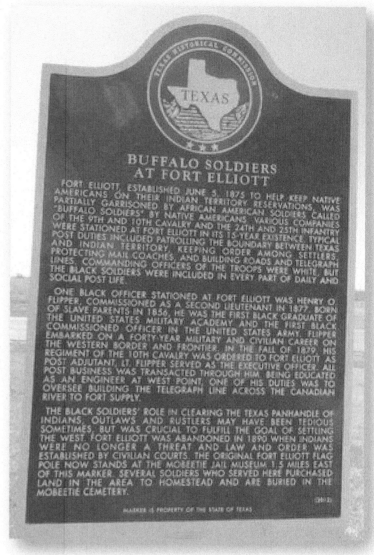

Black commissioned officer in the United States Army. Flipper embarked on a forty-year military and civilian career on the western border and frontier. In the fall of 1879, his regiment of the 10th Cavalry was ordered to Fort Elliott. As Post Adjutant, Lt. Flipper served as the executive officer. All post business was transacted through him. Being educated as an engineer at West Point, one of his duties was to oversee building the telegraph line across the Canadian River to Fort Supply.

The Black soldiers' role in clearing the Texas Panhandle of Indians, outlaws and rustlers may have been tedious sometimes, but was crucial to fulfill the goal of settling the west. Fort Elliott was abandoned in 1890 when Indians were no longer a threat and law and order was established by civilian courts.